To the love of my life—my beautiful wife, Suzie.
You have been the perfect mother of our children,
and now the best grandmother to our grandchildren.

For over 30 years, you have been my closest friend,
my lover, confidant, shrink, and even proofreader.
My life would not have been so blessed without you.

Next to Jesus, you have brought the most healing in my life.

ACKNOWLEDGMENTS

Humility has been defined as "realizing God and others are responsible for every achievement in my life."[A] How true! We are the sum total of all that has been freely given to us. It was never ours to consume, merely to cherish.

When Jesus cautioned, "...without Me, you can do nothing,"[B] He was inviting us into the life we were created for. He gladly admitted, "...the Son can do nothing of Himself, but only what He sees the Father do...."[C] This self-imposed restraint provided a doorway to heaven on Earth. Likewise, our surrender awards us "life beyond measure,"[D] peace beyond understanding,[E] and inexpressible joy in the here and now.[F]

"God can do anything, you know—far more than you could ever imagine or guess or request in your wildest dreams! He does it not by pushing us around but by working within us...His Spirit deeply and gently within us."[G]

Though I trust God has been this book's author and finisher, many other people have been involved in its creation:

My praying mother who raised me.

My brothers, Victor and Joseph, and sisters, Diana and Maria, who were some of the few bright spots in a pretty dark childhood. They remain wonderful friends.

My beautiful wife, Suzie, who was the best proofreader of all.

My beloved daughters, Deborah and Havilah, who, along with their mother, have been a constant reminder of what true wealth really is.

There have also been scores of people who have read and critiqued this book in its various stages of development. In addition, dozens of marvelously perceptive and wholesome Rock Interns— both young and old, plus members of our church family, have heard, read and received this: my life's journey.

Special thanks to Hans Bennewitz, who created a great cover; and to my personal assistant, Lydia Birks, who offered exquisite insights that rounded rough edges, often making me sound kinder than I really am.

But the premiere person who made this book possible is Natalie Eiferd, one of my daughters in the Lord. I have watched her grow into a brilliant, godly, mature woman who spent hundreds of hours turning my raw material into an exquisite feast that can transform lives. Frankly, her name could be on the cover as well.

For this selfless labor of love, Natalie, I will always be indebted to you.

Thank you.

Francis Anfuso
francis@rockofroseville.com

CONTENTS

I swear to you, I was just sitting there minding my own business when it happened. I was sitting on the front row of a weekend service, when the speaker on the stage startled me with these words: "Most of us spend our lives standing on the dock, looking out to the sea, waiting for 'OUR SHIP' to come in. We keep hoping for yet another in a long line of prayers we've prayed and expectations we've had to be answered or fulfilled, in the belief that THIS ONE will be the one to finally satisfy and make us happy. Meanwhile, Jesus is standing there on the edge of the dock, jumping up and down, trying to get our attention because He has arrived to BE and TO DO all that we are needing. Our SHIP has already come."

INTRODUCTION

When I heard those words, they pierced me to the core. I have always sought to make Jesus the preference for my whole life, but realized when Francis Anfuso was articulating the above words, the Lord was about to elevate my relationship with Him to a totally different level. If you were to read my journal since then, you would know what a difference that metaphor has made.

I've known Francis Anfuso for almost two decades and have watched him wildly succeed and mercilessly struggle. I've seen the words of this book become his life message and I've seen it significantly impact mine. Don't read this book—rather, journal and pray and reflect on it because its contents could truly 'mark' your life in ways that few have. If you're tired of being addicted to circumstances, then prepare yourself for a new addiction that you'll never need a support group for.

DR. DAVID LOVELESS
Senior Pastor of Discovery Church
Orlando, Florida

PROLOGUE

"...a righteous man...will have no fear of bad news;
his heart is steadfast, trusting in the Lord."

Psalm 112:7, NIV

I love books. I have been a reader much of my life.

Over the years, there have been times when I've read the prologue of a book and wondered why it was even there. The content hardly seemed important enough to be considered before reading the rest of the book. Sometimes, I have felt the book would have been better without the prologue, because nothing of value was added.
The prologue was, in fact, optional.

This prologue is not.

It has been included to explain how to get the most out of this book. I believe God wants to bring extraordinary works of healing to your heart as you read on.

The book is divided into four parts:

It is a deliberate sequence.

But, as I have come to realize, like so many other Christians, I spent the first 30 years of my Christian walk with the elements of this succession out of order. Subsequently, my relationship with God and the life He intended for me were out of whack.

I gave my heart to Jesus when I was 23. At the very beginning of my relationship with Him I was overwhelmed with His unconditional love. This was short-lived. I soon began to focus on MY love and appreciation for Him and for what He had done in my life. It would be three decades before I would once again revisit the place where God truly delighted in me as His son. My commitment to God had been based more on my performance than upon His total acceptance and love.

I strove to show God my affection and submission to His will long before I ever realized He really liked me. Sad to say, it would be a long time before I was able to fully embrace and completely enjoy my Christian walk. I became more of a worker than a worshipper; abandoned in my surrender, but without the security that comes from knowing God fully approved of my life.

In baseball, as in life, you need to touch first base before you can go on to second base. Each of these four sections represents a different base—they have been designed by God to be taken sequentially. Looking back over those first 30 years as a Christian, every day I would head straight for second base completely bypassing first. My relationship with God was backwards. Since then God has shown me a far better order.

Once I began to flow in the sequence God intended, I began to face every day with the highest expectation possible. As I have focused on this revelation of knowing His great love for me, my heart now embraces every circumstance that comes my way with joy and anticipation.

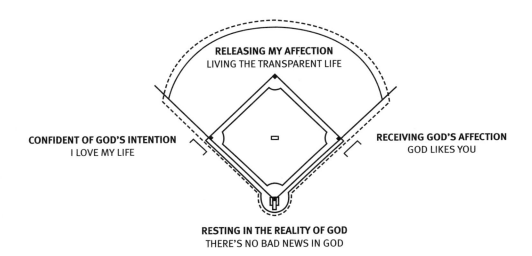

RELEASING MY AFFECTION
LIVING THE TRANSPARENT LIFE

CONFIDENT OF GOD'S INTENTION
I LOVE MY LIFE

RECEIVING GOD'S AFFECTION
GOD LIKES YOU

RESTING IN THE REALITY OF GOD
THERE'S NO BAD NEWS IN GOD

Sure, I still give God my affection and my obedience, but now it is as an affirmation of His endless goodness to me. Now, my works are effortless. What effort does a child need to make as his father is carrying him? None.

Trust, lie still, and enjoy the ride; life is so much better that way. I don't need a preference—He has already chosen the best for me. I don't need a plan—the Author of Life has it all figured out.

Because I now know Him, I trust Him. My commitment has become so much easier. It must be the yoke Jesus referred to when He said, "For My yoke is easy, and My burden is light."[H] God has the same desire for you. If you know Him, you cannot help but trust Him. God is showering His love and goodness down upon all of us. All we have to do is learn how to receive it.

From then on, your life will be **Perfectly** Positioned.

Francis Anfuso
April, 2007

RECEIVING GOD'S AFFECTION

CHAPTER ONE

IS THERE LIFE AFTER FAILURE?

WHEN DREAMS (ALMOST) COME TRUE

I walked into a dimly lit room on Sunset Boulevard in Hollywood, California. The producer of two of the most successful secular rock bands of all time, with more than 130 million albums sold, had assembled half a dozen of his creative team. He had invited me to present a 20-minute video I had produced describing a prospective multi-media youth tour. The 90-minute production was designed to reach millions of young people with a captivating, high-tech gospel message. As the video promo ended, the producer turned to me and remarked, "That was the best presentation of a project I have ever seen. I am very interested."

Our meeting had been set up at the request of the wealthy Christian owner of an estab-lished secular TV network. He had asked this top producer to critique the project and give his recommendations. The producer's conclusion: "If he *[the TV network owner]* doesn't provide financing for the tour, I will." It turned out that, though this producer was not a Christian, he had a praying sister who was. Later that day he showed my video to a Warner Brothers' Vice President, and once again, received a positive response.

I left the meeting ecstatic. The fact that it happened at all was a miracle, not to mention his overwhelmingly encouraging reaction. This had been a dream of mine for years. I had spent hundreds of hours with a team of creative people developing the tour concept, writing the script, and producing the video. Many other extraordinary contacts were made with highly capable Christians in the entertainment industry who were eager to use their gifts and resources to see this youth tour come to pass. Finally, it seemed that it was all coming together; everything I had prayed for—everything I had dreamed about.

Within weeks, the rock band producer flew to meet with a renowned Christian TV personality and myself to finalize the project. Lengthy discussions took place. Agreements were made. Everything seemed to be on course, until a Christian concert promoter advised the producer that there was not a large enough Christian market to make the tour viable.

It was a marvelous concept...

...a brilliant presentation!

...but too small a market!

Suddenly, everything I had worked so hard to see happen was taken away. It was over! I was in shock! How could God have allowed all of these remarkable meetings to take place and not bring the project to completion? I was totally unprepared for this jarring turn of events. And yet, this had not been my first experience with the "left hook from nowhere." On two other occasions I had been perfectly set up for massive disappointments.

Several years before, I had been given the opportunity to pitch a movie project I had been working on for ten years to an executive for the most well-known Christian film distributor in America. It received his enthusiastic endorsement, calling it, "the best distribution process for 35mm films he had ever seen." Yet despite the glowing reports, only a short time later, I realized the movie project would not be funded. In the end, it too, went belly up.

A few years after this ill-fated movie venture, I began developing a TV show for a top Christian musician. It was full of edgy concepts and innovative ideas. Once again, I threw my heart and soul into the preparation, pouring many hours into its development. The vision for the TV show was embraced; the show was successfully produced; but I was not involved. Here again, I was completely devastated and utterly traumatized. I would not soon recover. I had yet to learn the secret of living in contentment no matter what my circumstances were.

PEELING MY HEART OFF CLOSED DOORS

Once, while visiting with friends, I watched a seven-year-old boy run in and out of the house all afternoon. As the day wore on and the temperature dropped, the boy's mother decided to close the sliding glass door leading into the back yard. Somehow the little guy didn't notice, and a few moments later, going 50 mph, he smashed into the invisible barrier. He didn't just fall backward, he was propelled backward. He hit the glass so hard, I thought, "He's dead! There's no way he could have survived unscathed!" But much to our amazement, a few minutes later, with his nose somewhat readjusted, he was up and about, though moving much more gingerly.

I HAD YET TO LEARN THE SECRET OF LIVING IN CONTENTMENT NO MATTER WHAT MY CIRCUMSTANCES.

After each of my media projects died a slow death, I felt exactly like that battered boy. Having hit a brick wall with the "pedal to the metal," the wind didn't just leave my sails; God forcibly removed it. My heart sank in disbelief as I tried to grasp the unexpected turn of events. I was completely at a loss. Why had God consistently shown His hand of favor in each venture? Why would He allow me to invest so much time and energy on each of these worthwhile projects if He didn't want them completed? Why would he have me pray and see my prayers answered, only to ultimately watch the endeavors melt into oblivion?

Frankly, it seemed unspeakably cruel.

With each of these projects I stood waiting, as a faithful sentry, by open doors of opportunity only to have them abruptly slammed in my face. Yet, I refused to believe these shut doors would remain closed forever. The remarkable miracles I had seen God perform in two projects in particular seemed to refute that possibility. So I continued to stand outside the doors and wait for them to reopen. The waiting turned into years. In the end, I would accept the inevitable: these endeavors were on life support and I would have to pull the plug. I had to let my dreams die, walking away both shaking my head and shaken to the core.

I could only conclude: the greatest miracles I had ever seen took place in projects that God never intended me to complete.

Try filing that one away.

It would take me years to fully process what had gone on and come to terms with God's ultimate intention for each of these life-altering situations. Even though today I am completely at peace with the death of those projects, in the past it was not always so. It seemed not only out of character for God to allow such mixed messages, but emotionally criminal. I was convinced my appeal to a higher court in heaven would most assuredly render a different verdict. But, for what seemed an eternity, my petitions were unanswered.

I COULD ONLY CONCLUDE: THE GREATEST MIRACLES I HAD EVER SEEN TOOK PLACE IN PROJECTS THAT GOD NEVER INTENDED TO COMPLETE.

I have come to believe that "onward and upward" is in fact a non-biblical perspective. Though somewhat overstated, "onward and downward" would be much closer to the truth. "Before honor is humility."[1] God always defaults to what is ultimately in our best interest, and therefore has no intention of fulfilling all of our dreams. As the One who shaped and fashioned our inner needs, why would God fulfill a dream He knows is inherently unfulfilling? It has taken me half-a-lifetime to realize that His commitment is to fulfill His dream for me, which is infinitely better, though inevitably hidden from my eyes. "It is God's privilege to conceal things and the king's privilege to discover them."[2]

God's motive in this high-stakes game of hide-and-seek is pure and purposeful, though our experience on earth can be, at times, extremely painful. Many who have gone through unexplainable tragedy, often arriving at a life-altering crossroad with a broken heart, have come to a far different conclusion about the motive of God. One songwriter summed up human existence with this rather bleak assessment: "Life sucks, and then you die." How heartwarming! Though this statement may contain a small measure of truth, it by no means accurately portrays what life is about. God is not some cosmic killjoy getting His jollies out of pulling the wings off of helpless humans. In fact, quite the opposite is true. It is impossible for a blameless God to do anything but good.

When I was about ten years old, one of my great adventures in life was catching large bullfrogs. I loved the thrill of sneaking up behind them and then, moving at light-speed, plucking them out of the water with one fell swoop. Their skin felt so funny; so rubbery and slippery, covered with strange bumps. But, however long the hunt took, my exploits with bullfrogs always came down to catch and release.

Except on one tragic occasion.

One day, when I caught a really big bullfrog, I had the bizarre thought that it would be fun to methodically peel off his skin and see what was underneath. Everything seemed to go fine until I dropped the skinless frog back onto the hot sand. Only then did I fully realize the tragic mistake I had made. In horror I stared at the hapless victim now shrouded in sand. His life was soon over. I had, for all intents and purposes, killed him.

What started out as a neat idea turned into an ordeal I desperately wanted to reverse. Incapable of devising a plan to get his skin back on, I could only watch the doomed frog writhe in pain. Finally, unable to bear it any longer, I walked away feeling terribly sick inside. Forty-five years later I'm still embarrassed over what I did to that poor little frog.

Life is full of situations we wish never happened; setbacks and failures are as common to each of us as hiccups and headaches. Many of them are self-inflicted, while others are part of the script we have been given. Only with God's help can we properly respond to them, living—and eventually dying—in peace. Fortunately, God seems to take special pleasure in showing His power through our mistakes and weakness. The greatest lessons in life are primarily the result of learning to respond properly to what we perceive as failure or loss. Looking back now, I wouldn't change a thing, even though my perceived failure was so devastating at the time. I see now that God is able to use even failure for my good as I continue to trust Him.

LOUSY TIMING, PERFECT MOMENT

When my wife, Suzie, and I had been married for just nine months, I went to Montreal, Quebec to film during the 1976 Olympics. A small film crew and I traveled from California to film Christians publicly sharing their faith outside Olympic venues. God had provided thousands of dollars and the right personnel for the project.

The day before the Olympics were to begin, I called home to share with my wife how well everything seemed to be coming together. Suzie, who was three months pregnant, had visited the doctor that day and had been told, based on the physiological symptoms occurring in her body, she was probably having a miscarriage. The news was jarring. We prayed and I offered to take the next plane back to California, but she insisted I stay. My courageous wife, knowing how important the filming was to me, was resolute that I did not need to return home and that she would be fine.

Hanging up the phone, I prayed with the other members of our film crew for God's direction. I am so grateful that at such a critical moment godly men surrounded me. After much prayer and discussion, it was obvious to everyone that my priority was to catch the next plane home to be with my wife.

On the day the Olympics started and filming began, after months of grueling preparation, I found myself boarding a plane—doing the right thing—but hating every minute of it. I was mad. I loved my wife, and wanted to be there for her, but why did God have to pick one of the most important events in my young Christian life to ask for my obedience? His timing seemed, to say the least, really lousy!

Trying to keep a positive attitude as the other passengers were boarding the plane, I mechanically opened my Bible and began to read. It was a struggle, but I knew it was exactly what I needed, especially at that moment.

Suddenly, a deep male voice interrupted my train of thought, "Excuse me!" I looked up to see a large, distinguished, middle-aged black man, dressed in an African shirt and hat. After an ever-so-brief greeting, he slid past me and sat in the window seat. I returned to reading my Bible.

Shortly after takeoff, he turned to me and inquired, "So you're reading the Bible, huh?" At that moment I barely felt emotionally stable enough to read the Bible, much less carry on a conversation about it. I shot back a lifeless, "Yeah," and immediately put my head back down, hoping he would not have a follow-up question.

Over the years, I have had the privilege of leading many people to Jesus on airplanes, but that morning I was depressed and struggling to keep my heart in a healthy place. Normally, I would have welcomed a conversation, especially one about the Bible, but I was in the process of experiencing two of the biggest setbacks of my Christian life, and the last thing I felt like doing was chatting with a stranger.

The man, much to my immediate displeasure, didn't seem to notice my reluctance. Instead, he asked another question about the Bible. It seemed inevitable—I was headed for a conversation about God whether I felt like it or not. At first we began to talk rather haltingly, but he was genuinely interested and soon we were in the middle of a deep discussion. I shared what Jesus had done in my life and I could see he was being impacted. He told me his name was Archie Moore. Two hours into our conversation, I moved over to the middle seat. Archie expressed a sincere desire to receive Jesus, and so I led him in a prayer as the plane was touching down in Chicago.

Though my knowledge of him was sketchy at the time, I found out later he had been the former Light Heavyweight Boxing Champion of the world who holds the all-time knockout record. He even fought, and almost defeated, the legendary Rocky Marciano for the Heavyweight title. "Archie Moore was the oldest boxer to win the world's Light Heavyweight crown, and is believed to be the only boxer to have boxed professionally in the eras of Joe Louis, Rocky Marciano and Cassius Clay/Muhammad Ali. He was one of a handful of boxers whose careers spanned four decades, and he had a final record of 186 wins, with 145 official knockout wins."[3]

Once inside the airport terminal, I gave Archie a hug and said goodbye. He had just left when a young woman approached. She identified herself as a Christian who had formerly been a nightclub singer. She exclaimed that when Archie first walked on the plane she had recognized him and believed that God had providentially seated her directly behind me. Throughout the entire flight she had been fervently interceding for us and wondered why I had moved over to the seat next to Archie. As I told her he had prayed to receive Jesus, we rejoiced together in the airport. It was a wonderful moment.

How ironic! Having just been knocked out of filming at the Olympics, I just had the privilege of leading to Christ a future Hall of Fame boxer with the most knockouts in history.

I left the plane more at peace than I had been in the previous 24 hours; humbled that, even in the middle of my struggle for understanding, God could still use me to impact the life of this man. It had been less than three hours since I boarded the plane discouraged and dejected. Now, halfway home, I was flying high, having obeyed God and seen almost immediate fruit. There was life after failure!

On my second flight from Chicago to Sacramento, the Lord once again providentially sat me across from a wise and insightful nurse. For the next three hours I was able to ask her medical questions and learn more about the implications of a miscarriage. Though I was still somewhat bewildered and lacking in understanding, God had anticipated my every need! He did not forsake me, reject me, nor abandon me, but rather guided me to a new level of establishing priorities that would provide a healthy foundation for the rest of my life and marriage.

Because I was away filming the day after Suzie's disconcerting doctor's appointment, she had gone to stay with her parents for emotional support. I knew she was not expecting me to return so soon. I decided not to call, but to surprise her. A friend picked me up at the airport and drove me out to her folk's cattle ranch. She was totally shocked to see me standing there with flowers. Bursting into tears, we hugged and cried. It was a very moving moment. Even her dad, an atheist who rarely showed emotion, choked up when he greeted me and, looking into my eyes said, "Son, you did the right thing!"

I have no doubt, many years later, when Dad finally gave his heart to Jesus, that some of the first seeds of trust were sown on that fateful day. As her father, he didn't care if a video of the Olympics was made or not. But what he did care about, and what he did see, was that his daughter's husband was willing to give up even the most important thing he was doing to come to her aid. People will see far more of God in us by how we respond to failure, than to success.

Suzie had the miscarriage. It was a sad and painful loss, but a gigantic statement had been made. A pillar was put in place that remains steadfast throughout over 30 years of marriage. Wherever I am in the world, whatever work I am doing, if Suzie needs me, I will drop everything else and come to her side. One year later, God graciously gave us two beautiful, identical twin daughters. For God so loved… He gave….

The lowest moment in my early Christian life now stands as a signpost pointing to a better future. So too, for all of us, if we will obey God at these pivotal moments when we don't understand, He will give us "…beauty for ashes, the oil of joy for mourning, the garment of praise for the spirit of heaviness; that *[we]*…may be called trees of righteousness, the planting of the Lord, that He may be glorified."[4]

WHY GOD?

Whenever you find yourself wondering why something is happening, realize it is never a coincidence. It is invariably God working in you, giving you the desire to obey Him and the power to do what pleases Him.[5] Actually, *why* is typically the wrong question; *what* is the word we should be asking. "God, what are you trying to show me in this situation?" The situation, no matter how bleak, is not a mere accident; it is God at work, even using what Satan meant for evil. If we love Him and are committed to doing His will, He promises us that all things that happen will work for our good either on earth or in Heaven.[6]

At times, even those who felt called into full-time ministry have encountered impenetrable walls and were forced to detour from their original objectives. Sometimes these barricades can be from the devil. Paul, the apostle, wrote, "We wanted very much to come, and I, Paul, tried again and again, but Satan prevented us."[7] But more often than not, they are divine diversions; in-flight adjustments by our Commander-in-Chief.

A young married couple felt called to the mission field yet encountered a similar wall. Having been accepted by a mission organization, they just needed to pass a medical exam to be on their way. But, to their great dismay, the young wife was found to be physically unfit for the African climate. Heartbroken, they returned home and asked God for understanding in the matter. After much prayer, they resolved that if they could not go overseas themselves, they would make as much money as possible in America to spread the gospel elsewhere.

With missionary hearts, the young couple took over a small side business from the husband's father, making unfermented wine for communion services, turning it into a tremendous success. During their lifetime they gave vast sums of money to mission fields around the world. Their last name, by the way, was Welch, of Welch's Grape Juice fame.

THE ROAD TO HOPE

The words of the Apostle Paul have helped me on many occasions during my times of setback and failure. "We rejoice in our sufferings," he writes, "because we know that suffering produces perseverance; perseverance, character; and character, hope."[8] Working this spiritual equation backwards we find that if we lack hope, it is because we lack character; if we lack character, it is because we lack perseverance; and if we lack perseverance, it is because we have not responded properly to the trials and tribulations that face us. You don't get character by sitting in a hot tub eating ice cream. Character is only developed through struggles. Shakings are essential to life. We must go through them in order to experience "the removal of those things that are being shaken, as of things that are made, that the things which cannot be shaken may remain."[9]

It has been rightly said, "God always gives the best to those who leave the choice with Him." If we remain steadfast, confidently embracing God's providential plan, the final chapter of our lives will reveal His infinite wisdom and matchless destiny. Only He can take a shattered dream and multiply its potential a hundredfold.

IN CASE OF FAILURE, READ THIS!

Failure is an inevitable part of life, but we still have a choice as to how we will respond to it. We can choose to hide our failures and weaknesses from others out of embarrassment and fear, or we can choose to view these times as opportunities to see the areas in our lives that still need work. Embarrassment alone isn't enough to drive us to change. It is not until we get truly desperate that we will be sufficiently motivated to pursue changing our lives.

Embarrassment is merely the first stage of conviction. When we see areas in our lives that are out of control we feel embarrassed, but that is only the beginning of the sufficient provocation needed for change. Embarrassment is a junior stage of conviction—actually a baby step. People live and die embarrassed, but never really change. Expressions such as, "I know I shouldn't do it, but I do!" or "It's a horrible habit" merely gloss over an underlying lack of dedication to change. In Luke 9:45, the disciples "...were embarrassed to ask him [Jesus] what He meant."[10] Embarrassment brought about no eternal change. They were not yet ready.

The next stage of conviction is being fed up. When we are fed up, we no longer try to hide our failures; we attempt to fix them ourselves. Here again, though a person may be sick and tired of acting a certain way, being fed up will only produce depression or anger, but not a lasting change in behavior. A disciple is a whole-hearted follower of Jesus Christ. Jesus affirmed this when He challenged, "So likewise, whoever of you does not forsake all that he has cannot be My disciple."[11] Partial commitments produce insufficient results.

What is needed is a departure from conventional wisdom. We can live and die both embarrassed and fed up, and still see no tangible alteration of our behavior. Until we see our departure from sin as a life and death issue, requiring a desperate response, we will never rise to the level of concern that facilitates personal transformation. It isn't until we reach the final stage of conviction—desperation—that we will see the change in our lives we truly desire. We have to be desperate for God in order to be yielded to Him. The psalmist cried out, "I'm in trouble. I cry to God, desperate for an answer...."[12]

EMBARRASSMENT ALONE ISN'T ENOUGH TO DRIVE US TO CHANGE. IT IS NOT UNTIL WE GET TRULY DESPERATE THAT WE WILL BE SUFFICIENTLY MOTIVATED TO PURSUE CHANGING OUR LIVES.

Without embracing God's perspective, we will eventually fall into deception. God's not trying to change our circumstances; He's trying to change our reaction to them.

If the only way we learn is by making mistakes instead of being dedicated to change, then we are destined to become an ugly mass of scar tissue. The Word and the Spirit of God purpose to guide us into truth and to spare us the heartbreaking anguish of serious failure. If we only learn by being enrolled in the School of Hard Knocks, then we will experience the way of the unfaithful, which is unnecessarily hard.[13]

How does this progression of thought take place? Sin first begins in our thoughts, then thoughts become deeds, deeds become habits, habits form our personality, and ultimately, our personality shapes our destiny. In a similar way, if we don't stop evil desires in the thought stage, eventually they will manifest themselves as deeds, which sooner or later become habits, gradually overtaking our personality until, in the end, they establish our destiny. "Then the evil desire, when it has conceived, gives birth to sin, and sin, when it is fully matured, brings forth death."[14]

WITHOUT EMBRACING GOD'S PERSPECTIVE, WE WILL EVENTUALLY FALL INTO DECEPTION.

With God's power we can stop thoughts before they become deeds, and deeds before they evolve into habits. By breaking this cycle, we will live life flourishing in the oasis of God's personality and destiny.

Many Christians, leaders included, are paralyzed by fear of failure. They would rather debate and analyze than begin to do something—anything. It can be overwhelming to look at all of the failures in our lives and begin to learn from them. But as Hudson Taylor, the great missionary to China, said, "I have found that there are three stages in every great work of God. First it is impossible. Then it is difficult. Then it is done." I have been amazed over the years, as I have seen how faithful God has been to bring calm to chaos, and understanding to the devastations of my past.

THE CURE IS IN THE DISEASE

My aged mother often said, "Before you can appreciate the good, you have to experience the bad." Though perhaps imperfect in her theology, this wise lady had tasted enough of life to know something of its sequencing. Just as pride comes before destruction,[15] and humility before honor;[16] so too, we must know we are lost before we can be eternally saved. As with bad and good, failure must be realized before success can be appreciated. In a sense, the cure and the disease are inexorably linked.

Here is a perfect analogy elaborating on this profound principle. In order to provide protection and immunization from certain diseases, vaccines are developed which contain weakened or dead microbes of the kind that actually cause the disease in the first place. These inoculations stimulate the immune system to produce antibodies, which in turn fight the disease.

Jesus became sin for us in order "that we might become the righteousness of God in Him."[17] He chose the reproach of failure in order to secure everlasting success for those He loves. He allowed all of the bad that had ever been perpetrated by mankind to not just be placed at His own feet, but to be fully credited to His account. Christ's lowest moment became the launching point for our highest.

Will you willingly embrace the inevitable challenges of life that are, in fact, divinely prepared appointments with destiny? Will you allow God to renew your mind and heal your misconceptions of all that has transpired thus far? We have all misjudged God and His purpose for us. We have all given up too quickly. Our rescue is at hand. If we will but wait, hope and believe.

TRAGEDIES REDEEMED

A fishing fleet left a small harbor in Newfoundland and was caught in a terrible storm. When night came, the ships were scheduled to return home, yet none of them did.

All night long, the mothers, wives, and children of the fishermen walked the shores looking for some sign of their loved ones, praying tearfully that God would bring them back safely. Adding to their anxieties, one of the homes in the village caught fire in the middle of the night. Since all of the men were gone, it burned to the ground.

But as morning dawned, the entire fleet of ships sailed safely back into the harbor. All of the villagers rejoiced when they saw their men safely home, except the woman whose home had burned down. Approaching her husband with grief written across her face, she cried out, "We are ruined! Our home and everything we had were destroyed by fire."

Her husband, however, just shook his head. "What are you saying? Thank God for the fire!" he exclaimed. "It was the light of our burning home that guided the whole fleet into port."

Yes, in this world we will have tribulation. But Jesus says, "Be of good cheer; I have over-come the world!"[18] He has overcome the disasters of life. He has overcome the sin that infected us; and if we will but trust Him—and Him alone—we are destined to be overcom-ers as well.

REDEEMING THE UNREDEEMABLE

Looking back over the 23 years of my life before I met Jesus, I see a trail of self-gratifying choices which inflicted much hurt upon many of those around me. I used my God-given gift of persuasion to open the hearts of women, enticing them to give up their sexual purity. I fathered two children, which were later aborted. I persuaded scores of others to enter a bankrupt drug culture, rebel against God, family and society, all as I simultane-ously sank into my own caverns of self-deception. How many of those I led astray are still reaping the consequences of my treachery and sin? I am even now saddened to think about it. There was much to be ashamed of, and forgiven for.

But none of my fast talk could prevent me from reaping what I had sown. Breaking in-nocent hearts was the prelude to my not-so-innocent heart being broken as well. The accumulation of pain I had inflicted upon others came crashing down and nearly took my life during a six-month suicidal meltdown. I was on a collision course with death.

I will always be eternally grateful for a persistent, praying mother trusting in a gracious, merciful God. Even during my pre-Christian years there were a few situations that were miraculously redeemed by God after I became a Christian. There was life after failure.

Six months before I received Jesus, I was hitchhiking in Honolulu, Hawaii. An accountant from New York City and his family picked me up. He had shoulder length hair and was dabbling in smoking pot; a poster child for a counter-culture wannabe. Always ready to convert people to whatever I was into, I had an intense half-hour conversation trying to persuade him to give up his materialistic ways and pursue a more down to earth lifestyle. It was a sincere and meaningful conversation that, frankly, had no eternal value.

A year and a half later, after becoming a Christian, I was driving in New York City. As I was about to enter the busy Long Island Expressway, I saw a hitchhiker on the side of the onramp, whom I decided to pick up. As he got into the car, I instantly recognized him. He was the same accountant who had picked me up a year and a half before in Honolulu.

We were both stunned. God's presence filled the vehicle and I was suddenly aware of the fact that Jesus had fully orchestrated this divine appointment.

The man had unfortunately taken some of my misguided advice, and had become a card-carrying member of the hippie subculture. For the next half-hour, talking at New York warp speed, I shared with this now captive audience my complete testimony of God transforming my life, as well as an impassioned overview of the gospel of Jesus Christ. The electricity in the car was palpable. We both knew our impossible rendezvous had been sovereignly ordained.

Though at that moment he did not surrender his heart to Jesus, our lives were both shaken by the magnificent and flawless plan of God. This was one of the few times in my life I was able to impact the life of someone I had previously damaged. I treasure it as a moment when God once again redeemed the unredeemable, allowing failure to be eclipsed by faith.

Over the years, I have now had countless opportunities to help thousands of people who have made many of the same mistakes I once made. There is not a sin I have committed that I have not had the opportunity to tell another person about. There is not a type of person I have deceived, whom I have not had the privilege of guiding into a saving relationship with the loving God of the Universe. There is not only life after failure; there is a redemptive purpose in every sin, every setback, and every heartbreak we have or will ever go through. The life of your dreams is just around the bend, and the fastest way to get there is obeying the will of God no matter how unfulfilling it may seem during the process.

SUMMARY POINTS

- The greatest lessons in life are primarily the result of learning to respond properly to what we perceive as failure.

- Failure may be an inevitable part of life, but we still have a choice as to how we will respond to it.

- God's not trying to change our circumstances; He's trying to change our reaction to them.

QUESTIONS FOR DISCUSSION

1. What is your personal definition of failure? What do you consider to be a significant failure in your life? Why do you consider it to be a failure? How do you think God perceives it?

2. In what ways did you respond to this life experience? In retrospect, how would you respond differently today?

3. How do you think God has used this experience to produce His character in your life? How is God currently using what you learned through this experience?

4. Over the last week, how have you failed? In what ways did you respond? How has God used this failure in your life?

5. After reading this chapter, has your perception of failure changed? If so, in what ways? In what other areas do you think God wants you to change how you perceive failure?

CHAPTER TWO

CLEARING UP YOUR PERPLEXION

INSIGNIFICANT FROM BIRTH

My twin brother Joseph and I were born at the height of our father's political career. He was in his mid-40s and was running for office, to which he was subsequently elected to five terms in the U.S. House of Representatives. Having twin boys, late in life, was not a pleasant surprise. Consequently, neither was his response to us. My natural insecurities were soon fed by unnatural abandonment. In time, a supernatural God would heal both.

Joseph and I were sent away to camp every summer from five years of age to 14. During the school year we lived in oppressively strict boarding schools from 11 years old on.

We never lived at home again. It left me with deep feelings of personal inadequacy, anger toward my father and absolutely no idea of who I was. What was it about me that my father disliked so much? Rejection and abandonment were my childhood playmates.

Each of us is born with an abiding sense of our own personal insignificance. We are herded like cattle through school lunch queues, grocery lines and traffic jams. Acne and peer pressure, or more pointedly, being ignored by our classmates, parents and those closest to us frustrate our quest for self-importance. Yet, beneath the surface is an enduring hope that we do have some value, even if it is not yet revealed.

When I was a young boy in boarding school, I lived for years in a large room with 75 other boys—row after row of beds and dressers. I can hardly think of anything more impersonal and depressing. During my six years in this oppressively authoritative institution, we were never allowed to talk with our classmates—in any dorm room, classroom, hallway, bathroom, or shower. It was the loneliest experience of my life. I hated every minute of it.

There were no "Good mornings," no "Good nights"; just whistles and threats. The priest in charge of our dorm wore a long black robe with a cross, but would drink beer, smoke cigars and curse at us. He reminded me more of Judas than Jesus. It was like having a prisoner in charge of a prison. Since the day I graduated, I have never seen one person I went to grammar school or high school with. The year I left, they closed the boarding portion of the school down. Frankly, now 40 years later, it is still extremely painful to even think about.

During those forsaken years, I was so desperate for love and affection that I would periodically get up before the other boys and go to a mass conducted in Latin, a language I didn't even understand. I would sit in these services, tired and bored to death, while all the other boys were sleeping, for just one reason. In order to be awakened for mass, I would tie a towel at the end of my bed. The priest, seeing I wanted to go to mass, and not wanting to make any noise to wake the other boys, would shake me for a few seconds. It was those precious moments of touch, even at the hand of someone I detested, that made it all worth it. I had been touched. Not in anger or correction, but I imagined because someone cared. It is embarrassing to write, but true just the same.

GROWING UP FRAGILE

God always gives His best to those who leave the choice with Him. Yet children, in truth, have few choices. For better or worse, other people direct most of their lives. When I traveled as an itinerant evangelist I realized how much absolute control my wife Suzie and I had over our children. On a number of occasions we had to wake our pre-school age daughters, Deborah and Havilah, hours before first light to begin a long journey across the country. We were always struck by how compliant our children were to our instructions. "Get dressed girls, we have to leave soon!" Like toy soldiers they would without question obey our requests, seemingly walking in their sleep. Were they confident we knew what we were doing? No, I think they were merely following instructions.

For a season in my childhood I submissively ate the meals life dished out. But eventually, a closer examination of the food caused my frustration to boil over. When it did, no one was spared, least of all myself. I blamed everyone for my misery. Yet in the end, my loving Creator had written a foolproof script for me; it was designed to heal my past, establish my present, and inspire me to run toward a future beyond my wildest dreams. I am so thankful for the wonderful family I now have.

All of my brothers and sisters are following God. My wife and I have had decades of a marvelous relationship that only continues to get better. Our beautiful twin daughters married godly caring men, and each had their first child a week apart. I have a church family that consistently inspires me as they lay down their lives for Jesus and one another. I am a truly blessed man!

A LITTLE PAIN GOES A LONG WAY

Though it is impossible to fully relate and empathize with another person's pain, a little of our own pain goes a long way. I am not naïve to think that there are many of you reading this who could easily say, "So, you think that's bad? Listen to this!" My heart has broken countless times as battered people have shared the gruesome events of their deformed childhood.

GOD WILL TAKE THE YEARS OF TURMOIL AND BROKENNESS, AND TRANSFORM TORTURED MEMORIES INTO BRIDGES OF HEALING AND HOPE.

Whether we like it or not, we will each have to look back long enough and deep enough to allow the Lord to heal us. If we refuse, then the abused will become the abuser, and the neglected will become the neglecter. I work with people every day whose childhoods were so painful from abuse and neglect that they have spent years blocking them out. But they must still look back, through the healing eyes of a Creator who was with them during every horrific moment. He will take the years of turmoil and brokenness, and transform tortured memories into bridges of healing and hope; not only for ourselves, but also for those He will send our way.

As Paul, the former persecutor of Christians, once wrote, "So when we are weighed down with troubles, it is for your benefit and salvation! For when God comforts us, it is so that we, in turn, can be an encouragement to you. Then you can patiently endure the same things we suffer."[19]

Our own hurts often keep us from seeing our hidden worth, which is not to be found in the high points of our life, but rather hidden under the rubble of our greatest pain. Only time, heat, and pressure can produce the most beautiful diamond. So too, the Master Surgeon, in making all things new, allows old things to pass away. "Therefore if any man be in Christ, he is a new creature: old things are passed away; behold, all things are become new."[20]

Though our struggles may at times seem pointless, the fruit of seeing life from God's perspective will last forever. The scales of Heaven, measuring everything in terms of eternity, will not miss an ounce of our true value. Though we think there is tragic waste in our lives, if we allow God to heal our hearts, the character being produced will far outweigh the pain suffered.

If you hear nothing else, hear this: character only comes from receiving the love of God. All attempts to change without first knowing how much God loves you will consign you to a life based on performance—what you can do—and not accepting what He has already done on your behalf. Without knowing God's love, our lives eventually become a lie, devoid of the fulfillment found only in knowing our Creator. If we reject God's infinite love, we will try in vain to remake ourselves into the image of this fallen world; realizing only too late it was all for nothing.

Every day, people exchange an eternity of significance before a loving God for a meager 15 minutes of fame beneath the shallow applause of an indifferent world. Receiving God's love would have given them all the value they would ever need. Instead, the sublime is traded for the mediocre—beauty for ashes.

A young boy in South Africa once swapped a costly diamond for a few toy soldiers because he was ignorant of what he had. Satan, the enemy of our soul, trifled away his own eternal value, and now attempts to devalue as many other eternal beings as possible. Once known as Lucifer, the anointed worship leader of Heaven traded the priceless for the meaningless, when the love of God was all he would ever need.

Why is receiving God's love and the eternal character that comes with it so important? Because, in the end, there is no secret in our heart that our conduct will not reveal. In the beginning, charisma might get you going, but it will take character to keep you going. Though character may be seen in the great moments of our lives, it is formed in the small ones. The real limitations in our lives are only in us and in our character, never in the heart of a loving God. He will gladly fulfill our heart's desire once we fully embrace what is on His heart for us.

Though we are all seduced and distracted by the temporary pleasures of earth (e.g., money, idols, fame, relationships, etc.), "eternity is in our hearts,"[21] and nothing else will satisfy. Nothing outside of God's promises and desires for us will bring the satisfaction we crave. My father had everything anyone could ask for—wealth, fame, family— yet without God what he sought after never fulfilled him. I refuse to pass on the lie. By God's grace, the curse has been broken.

CARRIED BY GREAT WINDS

The great philosopher Arthur Schopenhauer once said, "All truth passes through three stages. First, it is ridiculed. Second, it is violently opposed. Third, it is accepted as being self-evident." During my formative years I would mask the pain of being abandoned by my father with a casual

THE REAL LIMITATIONS IN OUR LIVES ARE ONLY IN US AND IN OUR CHARACTER, NEVER IN THE HEART OF A LOVING GOD.

indifference to his public distinction. But all of my vehement rejection of his disregard for my life only verified how important his approval really was. The Bible says, "The glory of children is their fathers."[22] The original Hebrew language implies that this glory is "an ornament to be worn in honor... for all to behold its beauty." Even when bitterness blinded me from seeing the beauty of my father's glory, the longing for it was always there. It left me consigned to a lifelong tension: longing for his affection, while rejecting how insignificant thinking of him made me feel. Young children are unable to differentiate between what is normal and healthy, and what is merely common and dysfunctional. Without being able to understand that difference, my broken bond with my father led to an inherent distrust of all authority. I detested the duplicity between his public persona and our non-existent private life. The painted smile couldn't conceal my inner rage.

When I was growing up, I found the hypocrisy within the religious institutions of my childhood comparable to the duplicity of my father. We were all smiles for political photo shoots, but all was not well in the Anfuso household. Not surprisingly, I eventually blamed God for the betrayal that suffocated my undefended life. Only after a dramatic personal conversion was this cycle of bitterness finally broken. Having been consumed by a life of anger and resentment, my spirit was at last jumpstarted and a healing relationship with Jesus began.

Now, over 35 years later, I can honestly say that I walk free from anger, bitterness, and resentment, having learned to forgive and release those who have hurt me. Because of God's miraculous healing in my life, I live a life of peace and joy, loving others with the freedom God had always intended for me.

I am reminded of an old Chippewa Indian saying that my twin brother Joseph once said greatly inspired him: "Sometimes I go about feeling sorry for myself, and all the time I am being carried by great winds across the sky." This saying encapsulates the skewed perspective many of us tend to have, not realizing it has been the grace of God that has carried us through each of life's tragedies. In the end, it is this self-absorption that keeps us from seeing what God is doing behind the scenes in each of our lives.

THE REACTION TO THE ACTION

How we respond to life is far more important than what happens to us. Two people can experience identical challenges, and yet respond in polar opposite ways. Some of the most potent and memorable examples of opposite responses are found in the Bible.

Elijah is known as one of the greatest prophets of all time. He prophesied that it wouldn't rain for three and a half years, and it didn't. He believed God would send ravens to feed him, and God obliged. He prophesied the miracle of God multiplying a single mother's food, and God did.

In the book of 1 Kings, Elijah asks a single mother (a widow), in severe poverty, to get him some water. While she is going to get it, he requests some of her bread as well. Have you ever had a family member do that to you? As you're going to the kitchen to get something to eat, they yell, "Hey, while you're up, could you get me a glass of water... and some bread... and a napkin... and a knife... and some butter... and jelly? Hey, why don't you just stay in the kitchen until all my needs are met?"

The widow's bread just happens to be her last meal. She answers, "...I do not have bread, only a handful of flour in a bin, and a little oil in a jar; and see, I am gathering a couple of sticks that I may go in and prepare it for myself and my son, that we may eat it, and die."[23]

The single mother's response is like asking someone, "How are you?" and having them retort, "Oh, I'm suicidal." What could you possibly say then—"Really, that's interesting! Were you born suicidal, or did you convert?" The mother's answer to Elijah doesn't indicate a very optimistic perspective of her life and situation. I'd say she was a cup-is-half-empty kind of person.

I had a bleak roommate in college during my hippie phase. He was a completely depressed soul. He never talked and pasted dark charcoal pictures that looked like moon craters all over his closet door.

I once asked him if he was enjoying reading a certain book, just to break the two feet of solid ice in our communication. He slammed the book shut and snapped back, "I wouldn't be on page 158 if I wasn't." The ice remained unbroken. I'd say he was a cup-is-completely-empty person.

After the mother reacts to Elijah's request, he then responds, "Do not fear; go and do as you have said, but make me a small cake from it first, and bring it to me; and afterward make some for yourself and your son."[24] Elijah is effectively saying, "I hear you—you're going to eat your last meal and die. That's great! While you're at it, I'll take two eggs over easy, hash browns, an English muffin and some waffles. Do you have real butter?" Elijah seems to be oblivious.

Do you ever feel that way about God? You are freaking out and you feel like all He's doing is sun bathing! Nothing could be further from the truth. Whether we understand it or see it, God has ordered our steps in the most marvelous way possible. The test is: will we trust what we cannot see? Frankly, will we trust God?

The Bible addresses this most clearly when it says, "Trust in the Lord with all your heart, and lean not on your own understanding; in all your ways acknowledge Him, and He shall direct your paths."[25]

The sooner we give up our addiction to understanding what we think is going on in our lives, the sooner we can rest in acknowledging and trusting God in the bleakest of situations. Only then can we experience "the peace of God, which surpasses all understanding."[26]

UNLESS WE ARE WILLING TO DO THE RIDICULOUS, WE MAY NEVER EXPERIENCE THE MIRACULOUS.

THE ACCEPTABLE YEAR OF THE LORD

One of the most refreshing revelations drawn from knowing God is realizing that there is nothing I have to do to make my life special. I cannot add to my uniqueness, nor can I diminish God's one-of-a-kind plan for my life. All of His intentions toward me far exceed my expectations and, contrary to conventional wisdom, I have never disillusioned God. Why? Because He has never had any illusions about me to begin with. He is fully aware of my assets and liabilities; my strengths and weaknesses.

More than anyone who has ever known me, God is fascinated with my life. This fact, if fully received, provides perhaps the greatest sigh of relief for those of us who have at one time thought we have disappointed God, believing the lie that we had to earn His approval. The truth is: God's seal of approval is on our lives from conception to the grave. As Romans 8:35 clearly states "...nothing can separate us from the love of Christ."

THE ROOT ISSUE

After the impoverished single mom tells Elijah she has no more food, he encourages her with the Word of the Lord, "For thus says the Lord God of Israel: 'The bin of flour shall not be used up, nor shall the jar of oil run dry, until the day the Lord sends rain on the earth.' "[27] It takes faith, both to say this and to hear it! "So she went away and did according to the word of Elijah; and she and he and her household ate for many days."[28] The widow had faith to obey the word of the Lord, and God miraculously provided flour and oil for her.

At one point Jesus, obeying the Father, stuck his fingers in a deaf man's ears. That was big, but what followed was bigger. Jesus then took spittle and, placing it on His own fingers, put it on the man's tongue because he could not speak either. Now, putting fingers in deaf ears and spittle on mute tongues may be just another day at the office for some people, but for most of us that level of obedience would set a world record. Unless we are willing to do the ridiculous, we may never experience the miraculous.

Was the single mom's life without incident from then on? Hardly. "Some time later, the son of the woman who owned the house became ill. He grew worse and worse, and finally stopped breathing."[29]

Now comes the bigger test!

She said to Elijah, "What do you have against me, man of God? Did you come to remind me of my sin and kill my son?"[30] What is the root of this comment? Something in her past is obviously unresolved. She is still feeling guilty over a past sin. This reveals a priceless truth: when things seem to go wrong, your reaction will bring to the surface what God is really trying to get at in your life. Whatever your challenging circumstance is, it is only the catalyst to get to the root problem.

The Queen Mary was the largest ship to cross the ocean in her day. When she was retired, the regal vessel was anchored as a floating hotel and museum in Long Beach, California. During the conversion process, her three massive smokestacks were taken off to be scraped down and repainted. On the dock, they each crumbled. Nothing was left of the three-quarter-inch steel plating from which the stacks had been formed. All that remained was more than 30 coats of paint, applied over many years. The steel had rusted away.

It is the same in life. Fixing surface problems will only work for so long; you have to get to the source of the problem. We all have emotional time bombs that can sabotage us. A few years ago in Germany, three construction workers were killed when they accidentally detonated a World War II bomb that had been lying dormant for over 50 years. Guilt, shame, and bitterness are lethal time bombs that, though they might seem dormant over time, eventually can (and will) explode.

FIXING SURFACE PROBLEMS WILL ONLY WORK FOR SO LONG; YOU HAVE TO GET TO THE SOURCE OF THE PROBLEM.

When the exasperated widow again questions Elijah, he obediently stretches out across the dead son and the boy is miraculously revived. God was not trying to torment her over past sins; He never does. He had chosen her desperate circumstances to reveal His loving heart toward her in an unforgettable way. It is the same in our own lives. God's motive is always pure. His actions are designed for our greater good; and His goal is always intended to bring healing and purpose to our lives.

HERE I AM, SEND SOMEONE ELSE

My wife and I lived in South Lake Tahoe, California for nine years while our identical twin daughters, Deborah and Havilah, were growing up. Tahoe is a majestic alpine lake at an elevation of 6,500 feet, located on the border of northern California and Nevada. It is 12 miles wide, 22 miles long, and extremely deep. In some places it is so cavernous the water looks like thick, dark ink.

Tahoe is particularly known for its great skiing, and even hosted a winter Olympics in Squaw Valley. During our time there, we actually saw it snow at lake level every month of the year. During the late spring and early summer, as the snow from the surrounding mountains melts, some of it runs off into the lake itself, keeping the water temperature in the 40s.

One year, our church family held a 4th of July picnic on the shores of the lake. No one that day was swimming. This particular year had been unusually cold, with snow on the ground well into May. Consequently, all of us were wearing sweatshirts, with a few hearty souls in shorts and bathing suits playing volleyball. The wind was blowing quite strongly out across the lake; people had to closely watch their picnic items so they wouldn't blow away.

As the day was drawing to a close and it was cooling off even further, I was standing on the shoreline with a couple of close friends from the church. I had known them for well over a decade. As we were talking together, one of my daughters anxiously ran up and pointed across the lake yelling, "Daddy, that's Kathryn!"

There, well out into the lake, was a tiny inflatable raft. Though difficult to recognize from such a distance, we could tell it contained the eight-year-old daughter of the couple I was chatting with. A grim look shot across the father's face. Under his breath he blurted, "Oh, my God!"

The wind had blown her raft into the lake, so Kathryn had floated out on another inflatable raft to retrieve the first. Once she reached the stranded raft, she had picked it up and held it in her arms, figuring she would somehow make it back to shore. But with the strong wind that day, the raft in her hands had become a sail. As we watched, she was pulled out across this frigid lake with absolutely no one around her.

Her father almost immediately sized up her predicament and began to yell at the top of his voice, "Kathryn, let go of the raft!" But Kathryn didn't want to lose the raft and held on anyway. Her father kept frantically shouting, and finally Kathryn did let go of the second raft. The force of the wind sent it tumbling end over end away from land. This only confirmed our fears—the situation was critical.

As I stood in between the terrified parents, I could almost hear each of our minds race to find a solution. There were no boats, no swimmers, and no one to look to for help. Now, having heard the father yelling, only a few of us were aware of the drama that was taking place.

The father was a large man, overweight for his size, and fully clothed. Though I am sure he was willing to respond, frankly, it would not have helped. The mother, on the other hand, was an athletic woman who had a bathing suit on under her sweatshirt and sweat pants. Without saying a word, and never for a moment taking her eyes off her helpless child, the mom slipped off her sweats and dove into the freezing lake.

Commitment had now eclipsed contemplation. She was, as they say in poker, "All in!" My mind continued to race; was this situation really as serious as it appeared? Was there some other willing soul who could join the desperate mother? But with only seconds having passed and only a handful of people even aware a crisis was occurring, that option did not seem likely.

One final, dreadful question flashed across my frantic mind, "If I go in, what if I die?" We had just been talking about how the day before the local newspaper had headlined, "Two Boaters Drown in Lake." Somehow, their boat had capsized, and they both died of hypothermia before anyone noticed. Death was a very real possibility in this glacial lake. With Kathryn already well out into the lake and continuing to drift away, there could be a point where the further a rescuer swam, the further she drifted, and then even the rescuers would drown.

Yet all of these thoughts were countered by my final conclusion: "I will never be able to live with myself if I don't do something!" If the mother was willing to die for her child, I had to be as well. I stripped off my sweatshirt and ran into the water.

Hitting the chilled water was like diving into fire. Knives pierced my entire body. It was absolutely freezing. A good swimmer, I began to tear up the water; however, at nearly 40 years old, I quickly tired, slowed down and finally began to dog paddle. As my legs went from being parallel with the water's surface to becoming perpendicular, my feet touched bottom. Much to my dismay, I was still in shallow water. What an idiot! I had spent my best strokes and lung capacity swimming when I could have been walking.

Even in a life and death situation, it is amazing how much we care about what others think of us. For a few dysfunctional seconds my mind wrestled with embarrassment. People had been watching me from the shore. Not only was I the second person to dive in, I had also terribly misjudged my use of energy.

Another minute and I had reached the end of the shallows. Once again, I put my head down and started kicking. I had caught a little of my breath, but was still quite weary. Before putting my head down again, I took one final glance at Kathryn. She appeared to be almost as far away as when I had stood on the shore. It was not a comforting thought. Nevertheless, it was the last one I had before swimming again.

After another 50 strokes, I was once more out of breath. I no longer felt like a rescuer—I was swimming to survive. My body was exhausted and freezing. I was now close enough to Kathryn to hear her hysterical crying. It helped to know I was not the only person horrified by our predicament.

When I swam past the fatigued mother she was gasping for air, but just as intent to rescue her daughter as she had been when she first entered the water. She would, if need be, give her life for her daughter.

I don't know if the wind died down, or changed direction, or if God transported us forward, but somehow we both made it to the raft.

The challenge was by no means over.

Now we had to go back. But this time I had to swim against the wind. Trying to reach a distant shoreline, completely worn out, pulling a raft, with the wind in my face, made the return trip feel even more frightening.

Much to my surprise and dismay, no one else had joined us in our rescue. The mother told me later that, if I had not joined her, she would not have made it back. Two are truly better than one.[31] Upon reaching the shallows, others walked out to assist us. The father's eyes filled with tears and his voice cracked with emotion. Even days later, he thanked me once again for helping save his daughter's life.

How would I have felt if I had given in to my first perplexing thought wars, and chosen to merely pray for the mother and child from the safety and comfort of the shore? I now believe the father would have gone in and probably drowned had I not entered the water first. Instead of watching a happy ending, the worst case scenario would have then unfolded before my eyes. What if I watched some of my closest friends die because I had done absolutely nothing to help them? Like many other occasions, I would have spent the rest of my life regretting my cowardice and indecision. What sends a chill down my spine even now was how perilously close I came to not going, and how desperately needed I really was.

The mother's commitment to save her child, far more than my own commitment, resembles the sacrifice Jesus made for each of us. I would have been elated if someone—anyone—had run past me and dove into the water. But though I would have been ecstatic at the time, had the incident ended in tragedy I would have realized I had forsaken those I loved.

"Then Elijah stood in front of them *[the children of Israel]* and said, 'How long are you going to waver between two opinions? If the Lord is God, follow him! But if Baal is God, then follow him!' But the people were completely silent."[32]

Since receiving God's love for my life, I have committed my heart fully to Him. No one else could have saved me but the God who created me, for only He was willing to pay the price of rescuing my tortured soul. His desire has always been for me to come to understand His marvelous plan for my life and to learn to accept that His way is best. May I continue to let go of the things I mistakenly think are important; the perplexions that take me further from the safety of the shore and His loving protection.

SUMMARY POINTS

- Though our struggles may at times seem pointless, the fruit of seeing life from God's perspective will last forever.

- If you hear nothing else, hear this: character only comes from receiving the love of God.

- All attempts to change without first knowing how much God loves you will consign you to a life based on performance—what you can do—and not accepting what He has already done on your behalf.

- Every day, people exchange an eternity of significance before a loving God for a meager 15 minutes of fame beneath the shallow applause of an indifferent world.

- In the end, there is no secret in our heart that our conduct will not reveal. How we respond to life is far more important than what happens to us.

- The truth is: God's seal of approval is on our lives from conception to the grave.

QUESTIONS FOR DISCUSSION

1. Did you feel loved and significant during your childhood years? Describe your experience. In what ways has that affected your life today?

2. What was your relationship with your father and mother like as a child? As a teenager? As a young adult? In what ways did you respond well? Not so well? In retrospect, how would you have liked those relationships to be different?

3. What does the statement, "All attempts to change without first knowing how much God loves you will consign you to a life based on performance- what you can do- and not accepting what He has already done on your behalf," affect your thoughts and feeling toward God? Toward yourself?

4. How do you think guilt, shame, and bitterness have affected your life? How has God's forgiveness of your sins affected you?

5. What has most impacted you in Chapter 2?

CHAPTER THREE

GOD LIKES YOU

"We are not first warriors. We are first a bride.
We are first lovers, and then we do the acts of war."
Mike Bickle, International House of Prayer

APOLOGIZING FOR MY LIFE

Whenever I go on vacation, I have come to the conclusion that the most restorative place for me—spirit, soul and body—is being around moving water. Rivers are good, waterfalls are great, but nothing compares to the ocean. Vast, powerful and captivating, the ocean washes over my whole being.

As a lover of Jesus for more than three decades, I have had many tranquil moments watching ocean waves at sunset, reflecting on the wonders of God. Most of the time, these moments have been the perfect therapy for my battle-weary soul. However, on occasion, I have ended up more apologetic than refreshed. My time of prayer would invariably conclude with, "God, I love you, and I thank you for loving me. You have blessed my life in so many ways. I am eternally grateful. But, God, as I look at my many shortcomings, I just want to say, I'm sorry. I know I haven't been all that You intended me to be. I know my character has at times failed and I just want to again say, I'm so very sorry."

At that emotional crescendo I would often begin to sob, devastated to think my life had not measured up to the way God wanted it to turn out. I found myself always falling short of my perception of God's expectation for my life, regardless of whether I was in a season of spiritual victory or setbacks. This prayer of apology always left me feeling inadequate and empty.

Even as I write these painful past feelings down, there is a part of me that wants to speak up and say, "That's right! No matter what you believe now, those feelings will always be accurate. God's perfect. You're not. Say you're sorry." It is a part of me I have refused to listen to for a long time.

Though this critical view of myself may in some neurotic way fulfill the letter of the law, it is by no means the truth. A healthy parent does not relish in his or her child's incessant apologies for not being the son or daughter they had hoped for. In the same way, God does not get joy out of me apologizing for my life. If, after failing to live up to expectations, the default emotion to surface in a parent and child's communication is disappointment, something is seriously wrong. There are three possible reasons:

a. the child's behavior was consistently and predominantly hurtful;

b. the parent's expectations were persistently unrealistic; or

c. the child was trying to live up to an unrealistic expectation that his or her parents never intended for him.

Throughout my life, because I never fulfilled my natural father's massive expectations for me, I assumed that God the Father must feel the same way. Now I know that, though I am a sinner and my sins have hurt God, my failures alone do not sum up my relationship with Him—far from it.

His Word promises that when we truly receive what Christ's death and resurrection have accomplished, we are forever separated from the consequences of our sins, including guilt, shame and condemnation. "As far as the east is from the west, so far has He removed our transgressions from us."[33] In truth, we will spend eternity focusing not on what we did wrong, but on what God did on our behalf.

None of us are capable of compensating for our past. Therefore, God in His mercy promises us, "...I, even I, am He who blots out your transgressions for My own sake; and I will not remember your sins."[34] Unlike each of us, God can make this claim and actually fulfill His promise every time.

1 John 1:9 asserts, "If we confess our sins, He is faithful and just to forgive us our sins and to cleanse us from all unrighteousness." Understanding the meaning of life has little to do with how much we love God, but everything to do with how much He loves us.

Jesus affirmed this truth when He openly confessed, "As the Father loved Me, I also have loved you; abide in My love."[35] There is nothing more tragic than being unwilling or unable to fully receive the love of God. He alone gave everything to demonstrate how much He loves and cares for us.

THE INTERNATIONAL HOUSE OF PRAYER (IHOP)

On August 15, 1999, God woke me in the middle of the night with a vision. I saw Christians worshipping and praying en masse. Having just heard that day about the International House of Prayer (IHOP) in Kansas City, I knew the vision was related to what IHOP was pioneering. IHOP began in May 1999 as an intercessory mission base intent on establishing continuous, 24/7 worship and prayer. That night, I wrote the vision down and sent it in a letter to Mike Bickle, IHOP's founder.

In the fall of 2002, just five years after pioneering a church in Roseville, California, called The Rock of Roseville, the Holy Spirit spoke clearly to my heart. We needed to establish a House of Prayer in order for us to see the fulfillment of the call on our lives. In response to this, in the beginning of 2003 we sent dozens of leaders from our church to IHOP. These trips would forever change our lives.

During our visits to IHOP, we spent countless hours basking in the wonderful presence of God. We also heard powerful teachings about God's fascination for us: how He longs for His sons and daughters, and how we, the Bride of Christ, captivate His heart. Over time, these teachings opened our eyes to see that God didn't just love us; He genuinely liked and enjoyed us immensely.

SETTLING FOR SECOND LOVE

Since inaugurating non-stop prayer and worship in September 1999, thousands have been drawn to IHOP, spending hour after hour soaking in the presence of God. During our weeklong visits in early 2003, as we spent many hours saturated in God's Spirit at IHOP, God did a revolutionary work in our hearts. I personally experienced a closeness to Jesus like I had not felt since I was a brand new Christian 30 years earlier.

In the deepest part of my being I sensed God's heart was completely accepting—with no disappointment or sense of failure—only the joy of a lost son being fully restored to his Father. All I could do was receive God's loving embrace, and as I did, something extraordinary took place.

For years, even decades, I had developed a pattern of expressing *my* love to God. Many times throughout the day I would say, "God, I love you," or "Thank you, Jesus, for loving and caring for my life." I had considered this my First Love relationship with Jesus. In reality, it was Second Love. His love for me came first.

The Bible says, "We love Him because He first loved us."[36] I had become so preoccupied trying to attain God's approval, I had lost sight of His unwavering acceptance. Actually, I had never fully realized the extent of His feelings toward me.

In time I learned to lean less on the commitment I have made to Jesus, and to bask more in the eternal Covenant He has made with me. John, the beloved disciple, again qualifies the essential sequence of love: "This is real love. It is not that we loved God, but that He loved us and sent His Son as a sacrifice to take away our sins."[37]

I HAD BECOME SO PREOCCUPIED TRYING TO ATTAIN GOD'S APPROVAL, I HAD LOST SIGHT OF HIS UNWAVERING ACCEPTANCE.

I now discipline my spirit and soul to receive His unconditional love for me. I reject any thought that conflicts with the ultimate thought: that God is madly in love with me. No matter what I have done or what sin I have committed. There is nothing I could ever do to make God stop loving me. My repentance and return to God does not reactivate His love for me. It was never deactivated. Even before I was born, His thoughts toward me were pure joy and gladness.

How can I fully love God if I don't know He fully loves me? As Jack Frost teaches, "God loves you the way you are, and not the way you think you should be." If I sense He is actually displeased with me, then others will eventually sense I am displeased with them. I cannot give more than I have received. I cannot pass on to my children more than I have, whatever it may be: love, peace, joy, forgiveness, mercy, kindness, or acceptance. Kind will produce kind. Acceptance will produce acceptance.

King David once wrote, "How precious [valuable] are Your thoughts about me, O God! They are innumerable!"[38] God sees us as precious, even priceless. Before we were born and throughout our lives, He continues to have an infinite number of positive thoughts about us. As a truly caring parent, He adores us.

The Bible teaches that God the Father loves us no less than He loves His Son Jesus. In the Gospel of John, Jesus said, "As the Father loved Me, I also have loved you; abide in My love."[39] Likewise in the words of Jesus, "...You have sent Me, and have loved them as You have loved Me."[40] Ever see a doting parent smile at their child? That's how God feels about us. God takes pleasure in the very thought of us. We make God smile!

THE GREATEST REVELATION I NEVER HAD

My heart began to soak on these life-transforming truths. I disciplined my mind to stop chanting, "I love you, God!" which seemed to beg the question, "God, do you really love me too?" As my soul focused on His unconditional love for me, I was captivated by God's heart. It sounds like a simple enough revelation, but one I frankly never fully grasped.

A few weeks after an eventful trip to IHOP, while spending time with our pastoral team overlooking the Pacific Ocean in Northern California, I realized my heart had been changed. Gone was the apologetic view of my sorry little life. I no longer felt the compulsion to close my prayers saddened by what I had not become. At last I realized there was nothing I could ever do to make God love me more. Likewise, there was nothing I could ever do to make Him love me less. His loving kindness toward me was unshakeable.

I am now fully convinced that God likes me, even though in my immaturity I do things He doesn't like and I know are wrong. God could not love me any more than He already does. He does not love me more when I am good, nor does He love me any less when I am bad. Even in my lowest moments God still likes me, and fully differentiates between who I am and what I do.

Like a good parent, His love for me is unwavering. The Bible says, He is the same "...yesterday, today, and forever,"[41] and "For I am the Lord, I do not change."[42] Therefore, if you have ever believed God loved you, or even liked you, He still does. He cannot change. He has not moved His affections from you. God likes you, all the time, just as you are; not based upon your performance, but based upon who He created you to be.

Mike Bickle sums this up so well: "God doesn't see us the way many of us see ourselves. He does not define us by our struggles, but rather He defines us by His passion for us and our longing to be a lover of God."[43]

WHOSE OPINION OF ME MATTERS MOST?
Before we can fully appreciate the fact that God genuinely likes us, we have to understand who He really is. We can't appreciate that God likes us if we fail to see Him as the kind of person we would want to like us. Does it really make that much of a difference what He thinks?

When I was a young Christian, there was a woman living in our community who personally knew Charles Manson, a cult leader and mass murderer during the 1970s. After some discussion and prayer, we decided to write Manson

> "GOD DOESN'T SEE US THE WAY MANY OF US SEE OURSELVES. HE DOES NOT DEFINE US BY OUR STRUGGLES, BUT RATHER HE DEFINES US BY HIS PASSION FOR US AND OUR LONGING TO BE A LOVER OF GOD."
>
> -MIKE BICKLE

a letter in prison, trying to share the love of Jesus with him. Within days he sent back a surprisingly lengthy response attempting to persuade us that he was the savior we were looking for, not Jesus. It would have been laughable, if it weren't so sad. Was it hard for us to reject Charles Manson's invitation to follow him? Not at all. I didn't care what he thought of me, because I thought so little of his opinion.

On the other hand, our Creator is the only person truly worthy of our complete allegiance and affection.[44] His thoughts about us are all that really matter. Do we know what God really thinks of us? Is He glad or sad, grateful or disappointed in whom we have become? The answer to this question will shape every dimension of our lives, and could not possibly be overestimated. We are God's sons and daughters. If we believe He is ashamed of who we are, we will walk in shame. On the other hand, if we believe God created us in His image and likeness,[45] then we can walk in confidence and security, knowing we are accepted by the One who matters the most. Not only does Jesus accept us without reservation, He willingly chose to give His life, so that we might have life.[46]

BOY IN A WELL

My older sister Diana has lived in Italy for over 25 years. A few years ago, a little Italian boy accidentally fell into a small well opening, feet first. It was thought the well had been sealed, though obviously inadequately. When the boy's mother went looking for him, she heard his anguished cries beneath her feet.

Word spread quickly, and in no time it was headlining the evening news. TV crews came from all over Italy to keep the country informed with constant updates. Efforts were made by police and fire to rescue the helpless child, but none were successful. Soon the boy, encased in mud with arms extended upward, had sunk so deep he could hardly breathe. Yet, the child persisted in calling out for his mother to come to his aid. A microphone was lowered and all of Italy could hear the boy's desperate cries.

Day and night TV coverage focused solely on the boy's plight; all other programming was cancelled. The nation watched, riveted to the abandoned well and the frantic child. At three o'clock in the morning, while watching the drama unfold on her television, Diana looked out her apartment window and could see lights on in most people's homes. It seemed the entire population was glued to the unfolding tragedy. Even the Italian Prime Minister came to the mouth of the well in an attempt to comfort the terrified mother and nation.

Finally, after many futile attempts to save the boy from certain death, a nationwide appeal was made. An adult, small enough and willing to attempt a headfirst rescue was sought. Soon, a double-jointed circus performer came forward and volunteered to risk his life. His thin frame was so agile he could bring his shoulders together until they touched.

As a praying nation watched, the courageous man with arms fully outstretched was pushed like a cork into the tiny well opening. His body had been coated with a lubricant to allow greater ease into the cylinder. The opening was so narrow, his undersized head barely fit within its diameter. Yet down he went, contorting his body to its limit, as the nation held its breath and watched.

Word spread that the contortionist had reached the child and grabbed ahold of him. As audio from inside the well continued to be broadcast, the cries of the rescuer could be heard as the boy was grasped but then slipped out of his hands. The child then sank out of reach and was consumed by the mire.

The exhausted and sobbing man was then pulled from the deadly well, barely recognizable beneath a layer of sludge. He, along with the distraught mother and many at the edge of the abyss, was inconsolable. The entire nation mourned.

The issue upon God's heart is not focused on our mistakes, but rather His absolute devotion and concern for our well-being. "For He made Him who knew no sin to be sin for us, that we might become the righteousness of God in Him."[47] Jesus was willing to enter the muck and mire of our tragic lives, with the full support of the cloud of witnesses and heavenly host.[48]

Though God "...desires all men to be saved and to come to the knowledge of the truth,"[49] the greatest tragedy of life is that despite His sacrifice, some will not. Nevertheless, the truth of God's unconditional love for us stands, as does His willingness to give His life so "...that we might live...."[50]

During World War II, Corrie ten Boom's Christian family hid Jews from the Nazis. When the Gestapo finally caught them, all were sent to the infamous concentration camp, Ravens-bruck. There, Corrie and her sister were separated from their father. Only Corrie survived. As the war ended, after ten months of incarceration, she was freed. Having seen and suffered unspeakable atrocities, Corrie later wrote, "There is no pit so deep, that God's love is not deeper still."

MISUNDERSTANDING THE LOVE OF GOD

Prior to the revelation of God liking me, I suffered from a glaring misunderstanding of scripture related to the love of God. Whenever I read about the love of God in the Bible, I would consistently think of my love *for* God. When I would read Romans 5:5, which says, "Now hope does not disappoint, because the love of God has been poured out in our hearts by the Holy Spirit who was given to us," I would think, "my hope will not be disappointed if I continue to demonstrate my love for God." My thinking was totally flawed. I now believe this scripture could more accurately be interpreted as "I can be hopeful in every situation because God's everlasting love continues to be poured out in my heart by the Holy Spirit."

With the revelation of God liking me, I came to the realization that the emphasis should never have been on my love for God, but instead always, and in every situation, on His love for me. There is an infinite difference between my capacity to hold on to God, and His commitment and ability to hold on to me.

Take a look at Jude 21: "Keep yourselves in the love of God, looking for the mercy of our Lord Jesus Christ unto eternal life." This verse encourages me that if I continue to receive God's love for my life, I will remain face to face with the eternal mercy of God found most evidently in the life and death of the Lord Jesus Christ. On the other hand, attempting to remain focused on my love for God will lead once again to a roller coaster of disappointment in my own imperfections.

During this season of my life, I continuously readjusted my thoughts to try to receive God's Word as He intended. I even had to discipline myself to *not* tell God I loved Him. My chanting "I love you, God!" had become a desperate

THE EMPHASIS SHOULD NEVER HAVE BEEN ON "MY LOVE FOR GOD," BUT INSTEAD ALWAYS, AND IN EVERY SITUATION, ON "HIS LOVE FOR ME."

means at trying to retain His acceptance. In reality, my expressing how much I loved God could not possibly have the same effect as first receiving His love for me.

Over time, as my heart was healed, I was able to more fully embrace God's overwhelming love for me. I began to express my love for God once again, but only after being fully saturated in His First Love for me. Oswald Chambers sums up this principle so well when he writes, "The only relationship God wants to have with us is based on love; if we refuse these terms there is no relationship."

RECEIVING GOD'S APPROVAL

How many young women have given away their emotions, their trust, their intimacy and even their moral purity, desperately wanting someone to love and completely approve of them? How many men likewise have done things they knew were wrong just to impress someone? Today's cultural seal of approval is centered on the applause of men, having a shelf life measured in nanoseconds compared to eternity. We can spend our lives endlessly attempting to derive our value from a fallen planet hurdling toward judgment, or we can choose to build on only what is consistent with God's Word and is guaranteed to last forever.

We see our immense value to God most clearly in the life of Jesus. Jesus began His earthly ministry at 30 years of age. When John the Baptist baptized Him in the Jordan River, a supernatural event took place that reveals the Father's heart for each of us. "...Jesus came up immediately from the water; and behold, the heavens were opened to Him, and He saw the Spirit of God descending like a dove and alighting upon Him. And suddenly a voice came from Heaven, saying, 'This is My beloved Son, in whom I am well pleased.' "[51]

There is no evidence in Scripture prior to this event that the Father had spoken audibly to Jesus during His first 30 years on this Earth. For His Coming Out party, God the Father had a special treat. He wanted everyone to know how proud He was of His Son, so He shouted from Heaven, "Hey everybody, listen up, this is My Son; and, 'You know what, Son? I really love You and am so very proud of You!'" The Father broke His three decades of silence to share two life-changing principles: "I love you and I am so very proud of you."

Most of us have never been overly concerned about whether the Father loved or was proud of Jesus. We all pretty much assume, "What's not to like?" But the love and approval the Father bestowed on Jesus is not reserved for Him alone. In Ephesians 1:6, the

Word of God promises us as well, "...He [God] made us accepted in the Beloved." The Greek word here for Beloved is agapao. It is derived from the same Greek word, agapetos used when referring to Jesus as Beloved in Matthew 3:17. Thus, we are accepted into the same Beloved family as Jesus.

In a very real sense, when our lives are surrendered to Jesus, the Father likewise speaks from Heaven to each of us, "Hey, listen up, this is My child. And you know what? I really love you and am so very proud of you!'" What a comfort to know we are as much loved and approved of by God as Jesus.

No matter what sins or mistakes we have made in life, it is essential that we fully accept this truth: God does not want to clobber us, He wants to crown us. "You shall also be a crown of glory in the hand of the Lord, and a royal diadem in the hand of your God. You shall no longer be termed Forsaken [Hebrew—destitute, refuse], nor shall your land any more be termed Desolate [Hebrew—devastated, wasted]; but you shall be called Hephzi-bah [Hebrew—a pleasure, desirable, a valuable thing, acceptable, delightsome], and your land Beulah [Hebrews—married, a wife]. For the Lord delights in you, and your land shall be married."[52]

The crowning moment of my life was the realization that I was no longer forsaken, devastated and wasted, but that my life was actually a pleasure to God, valuable, accepted, and a delight. I was created to be the Bride of His dreams, not the embodiment of His disappointment. What a relief! What a joy! We will never know the fullness of God's love until we experience failure and then realize He is still madly in love with us. "Thanks be to God for His indescribable gift!"[53]

SMILING WITH HIS SPIRIT

During the mid-19th century, a boy named Joseph seemed completely normal until age two when abrasions began to appear on his skin. They were the first swells of a violent storm that would envelope his fragile life.

Joseph had a wonderful, godly mother, but she died when he was ten years old. He was left with a cruel father and a bitter stepmother who hated him. Joseph's deformities worsened. He had massive feet, was unable to use one of his hands, and became deaf in one ear and blind in one eye. The malformation of his mouth made it almost impossible to understand him when he talked.

At one point, his head measured three feet in circumference, his right wrist 12 inches, and his right thumb five inches. Fungus grew all over his body giving him a hideous odor. As a teenager, Joseph was so deformed that while trying to sell products door to door, women would scream and even faint.

When Joseph was 15, his alcoholic father beat him so badly he was left unconscious and bleeding underneath the kitchen table. Sometime during the night, Joseph regained consciousness, crawled out from beneath the table, and quietly gathered a few belongings, leaving home for good. Unable to support himself, the dejected youth eventually found work in a freak show—billed as "Joseph Merrick—The Elephant Man." Because his skin looked like elephant skin, his handlers made up a story that, while pregnant, an elephant had attacked his mother.

One day, a doctor visited him and, overcome with compassion, placed Joseph in a hospital. The doctor later described Joseph as "the most disgusting specimen of humanity I have ever seen." During this period of his life, when one of the hospital attendants smiled at Joseph, he was so overcome by the kindness of this simple act that he broke down in tears saying, "You are the first woman I can ever remember who smiled at me."

During his long hospital stay, to the amazement of everyone around him, Joseph built incredibly elaborate cathedral-like structures using only one hand. He would sit and read the Bible, especially the Psalms, for hours. It was said of Joseph, "He could not smile with his face, but he learned to smile with his spirit."

At just 28 years of age, Joseph passed away, having lived a truly extraordinary life. In spite of overwhelmingly tragic circumstances, Joseph learned something that many people with far easier lives never do. He learned that God really liked him, and was able to live in the joy and peace that comes from this life-altering revelation. As I reflect on his broken life, I like to imagine he once read and believed the comforting words of King David, "...this I know...God is for me."[54]

No matter who we are or what we have done, whether beautiful or ugly, rich or poor, good or bad, loved or unloved, approved or rejected, we each must know in the deepest part of our being that there is a God who made us in His own image and likeness. A God who not only loves us unconditionally, but likes us so completely His heart smiles every time He thinks of us—and He thinks of us constantly.[55]

SUMMARY POINTS

- In truth, we will spend eternity focusing not on what we did wrong, but on what God did right on our behalf.

- Understanding the meaning of life has little to do with how much we love God and everything to do with how much He loves us.

- My repentance and return to God does not reactivate His love for me. It was never deactivated. Even before I was born, His thoughts toward me were good.

- The emphasis should never be first on my love for God, but instead always, and in every situation, first on His love for me.

- What a comfort to know I am as much loved and approved of by God as Jesus Himself.

QUESTIONS FOR DISCUSSION

1. How do you think God views your life? How do you view it? How do you think your view affects your perspective of God?

2. What does God feel about you when you are victorious? When you fail?

3. How did this statement in chapter three affect you? "The issue upon God's heart is not focused on our mistakes, but rather His absolute devotion and concern for our well-being."

4. What does having a "First Love relationship with Jesus" mean to you? How do you live out that relationship in your daily life?

5. How does the thought that God loves and accepts you just as much as He does Jesus affect you?

RELEASING MY
AFFECTION

CHAPTER FOUR

EVERYBODY WANTS A BREAKTHROUGH, BUT NOBODY WANTS TO DIE

DOCTORATE IN DEPRESSION

Much of my childhood was something I would rather forget. Once, when I was 15, the oppressive religious school I attended had a one-day retreat for my entire class. While there, each student was asked to spend time alone in a rose garden talking with God about His plans for our lives. It was the last thing I wanted to do! As far as I was concerned, God had ceased to exist. I figured if He wasn't the perpetrator of my miserable life, He certainly drove the getaway car.

Nothing could calm the fury of my hurt and hostility toward an absentee God. My reluctant stroll around the garden was short and bitter. At one point I told God, "If You are responsible for what is happening in my life, then we have nothing in common. This is my final conversation with You!"

And for seven years, it was.

How much mileage can you get out of blaming others for your life, whether it's people or God? Not much! At some point you will run out of gas, and realize you alone are responsible for how you choose to respond to life. Ultimately, the condition of our heart and mind is our own choice. I let my indignation over the massive amount of hurts blind my ability to see what God was actually doing in my life. I wanted freedom, but wasn't willing to pay the price. One day, I would learn to lay aside my selfish desires for a God who longed to give me greater understanding of His perfect plan and heal my broken heart.

ALWAYS GOING THROUGH IT... NEVER GOING UNDER

In the New Testament, the Apostle Paul was a revolutionary preacher who lived an extremely challenging life. He gave up much to follow Jesus, and though he continually met with seemingly insurmountable challenges, he refused to blame God for his difficulties. Unlike most of us, he did not allow himself to become angry or bitter with God because the conditions of his life were often miserable.

In the beginning of chapter 12 in the Book of 2 Corinthians, Paul is taken to Heaven and receives such mind-expanding revelations that he is never permitted to speak of them again. The apostle sees and hears so many lofty things, he is concerned he will be overcome with pride.

Paul plainly states, "And lest I should be exalted above measure by the abundance of the revelations, a thorn in the flesh was given to me, a messenger of Satan to [torment] me...."[56] Paul has gone from being elated about spiritual revelations, to begging God for help, "Concerning this thing I pleaded with the Lord three times that it might depart from me."[57]

Was Paul just a coward unwilling to fight his own battles? Not at all! He could take a hit as well as anyone who ever lived. In fact, in the previous chapter he lists just some of the greatest tests of his life: "From the Jews five times I received 40 stripes minus one. Three times I was beaten with rods; once I was stoned [being hit with rocks thrown by an angry mob and left for dead], three times I was shipwrecked; a night and a day I have been in the deep; in journeys often, in perils of waters, in perils of robbers, in perils of my own countrymen, in perils of the Gentiles, in perils in the city, in perils in the wilderness, in perils in the sea, in perils among false brethren; in weariness and toil, in sleeplessness often, in hunger and thirst, in fastings often, in cold and nakedness...."[58]

Paul was not some lightweight, unwilling to deal with hard situations. He was a gnarly street fighter who followed God regardless of the cost, yet he begs God to remove the thorn from his side. What was God's response to Paul's desperate pleadings? Did He

issue an edict to "stop the satanic tormenting?"
Hardly. God's response seemed to bring no immediate
relief whatsoever.

Paul wrote, "And *[God]* said to me, 'My grace is sufficient
for you, for My strength is made perfect in weakness.'
Therefore most gladly I will rather boast in my infirmities,
that the power of Christ may rest upon me."[59] In this case,
the original Greek word for *infirmities* means "feebleness
(of mind or body), a malady, a physical or psychological
disorder, disease, frailty, sickness, or weakness."

Paul understood that God's all-sufficient grace was being poured out. He then had one of the most astounding
revelations of all time. Paul was enlightened as to what
God was doing in his life, and was more than ready for the
challenge. He began to elaborate on what God has said,
and placed that new understanding as a permanent filter
guiding every dimension of his life.

I MAY HAVE MASSIVE NEEDS... BUT, NO MATTER WHAT HAPPENS, I'M NOT GOING TO FORGET THIS ONE THING: AS WEAK AS I FEEL, I WILL LEARN TO RELY ON GOD FOR STRENGTH.

With that new perspective in place, Paul's startling
response to the unrelenting challenges was, "Therefore
I take pleasure in *[Greek—think well of, approve, am
pleased with]* infirmities, in reproaches *[Greek—insults,
hurts]* in needs, in persecutions, in distresses *[Greek—
calamities & anguish]* for Christ's sake. For when I am
weak, then I am strong."[60]

Here is Paul's radical, groundbreaking perspective, "I'm
going to see God working in every situation of my life. I'm
going to think well of every circumstance. I may be sick,
hurt or insulted; I may have massive needs, persecutions,
distresses, calamities and anguish. But, no matter what
happens, I'm not going to forget this one thing: as weak
as I feel, I will learn to rely on God for strength. He will see
me through."

Because of this astounding, life changing epiphany, after being beaten and thrown in jail in the book of Philippians, Paul was able to affirm, "...I have learned in whatever state I am, there I will be content."[61] What a discovery! He is declaring, "My contentment has nothing to do with what is happening around me, and everything to do with what is happening inside me." Contentment is the result of our trusting God no matter what is happening around us. It is more of a decision than a consequence. Sounds like the antithesis of the victim mindset, and the dawn of a new era of personal responsibility. Paul had the breakthrough of a lifetime because he was willing to continually die to his own misconceptions of God.

IN-YOUR-FACE ATHEIST

My decision to walk away from God as a teenager set in motion a chain reaction of self-destructive behavior that nearly took my life. Over time, I fully degenerated into an adamant, in-your-face atheist. Whenever I met an outspoken Christian, I would openly mock his or her pathetic faith in the crutch they called "God."

In one college class, "The Bible and Its Influence on English Literature," I wrote a scathing term paper denouncing the truthfulness and accuracy of the Bible and the very concept of God. Making copies of the document at my own expense, I handed it out to anyone who would listen to my naive, judgmental tirades.

Then, during my sophomore year in college, I became strongly attracted to a girl voted the prettiest in her freshman class. Though I had never spoken with her, over the next two years my feelings for her escalated to the point of distraction. Desperate to find peace, I fled to Europe.

The university I was attending owned a majestic 12th century Abbey in Wroxton, England,[62] where undergraduates could study abroad for a semester. So, along with 50 other students from across America, I went to live in the summer home of King James I. There, we received instruction from Oxford University professors.

Though there were many incredible dimensions to this undergraduate program, the absolute low point of my six months abroad was my initiation into the personality altering world of drugs. In particular, I found the European variety of hashish—laced with opium—particularly potent and addictive. The last thing my overactive mind needed was a drug habit to exacerbate my inner pain, further magnifying my already neurotic, hyper-analytical personality. It was unfortunate that I turned a potentially once-in-a-lifetime experience into an "I wish I'd never done it" memory.

My European diversion ended with me taking my first hallucinogenic in Florence, Italy. While high on mescaline, I walked through the Convent of San Marco, where the Catholic monk Fra Angelico painted vivid depictions of the crucified Jesus on the walls of the residence. Out of my head on this mind-altering drug, I saw the blood literally pouring out of Christ's crucified body. I ran out of the convent and spent the next few hours in a filthy rundown hotel, watching my face melt in a bathroom mirror.

I have since visited the Convent of San Marco in Florence, and found the paintings of Jesus to be beautiful works of art. I knew it must have been a combination of the drug and the demons inside of me that turned my tour into terror.

CHALLENGING THE GREATEST

There are many occasions in life when we are unable to understand what God is doing. In the New Testament, John the Baptist was the prophet who went about fasting often and baptizing people in rivers. He was a privileged soul whom God designated to announce the coming of the Christ. Yet, like each of us, John at times struggled with seeing God at work in his life.

After Mary conceived Jesus by the Holy Spirit, she went to her relatives' house to visit Elizabeth (John's mother) who was also pregnant with John the Baptist. When Mary and Elizabeth greeted one another, John leapt in the womb as he came into the presence of the Son of God. From his mother's womb, John knew who Jesus was. As an adult, when John was baptizing in the Jordan River and saw Jesus coming, he said, "Behold the Lamb of God who takes away the sins of the world."[63] John recognized Jesus as the Son of God, both in the womb and as an adult.

Some time later, when John was in prison and about to be beheaded, he sent a few of his disciples to ask Jesus, "Are You the one, or should we look for another?"[64] Is John suffering from amnesia? Or, frightened by the eminency of his death, is he questioning, "God, where are You?" When Jesus hears of John's inquiry, He doesn't reprimand or think ill of him. Instead, Jesus gently replies, "Go and tell John the things you have seen and heard: that the blind see, the lame walk, the lepers are cleansed, the deaf hear, the dead are raised, the poor have the gospel preached to them."[65]

Who was John the Baptist anyway? Was he some unstable, erratic eccentric, or one of the most solid and focused prophetic voices in all of human history? Jesus once said of his cousin John, "...among those born of women there is not a greater prophet than John the Baptist..."[66] John was at least tied for first amongst the premiere prophets of all time. And yet, in the hour of his greatest temptation, John may have questioned if Jesus really was the Messiah.

WITH PERHAPS THE EXCEPTION OF THE JOSEPHS AND DANIELS, IT IS HARD TO FIND A PROPHET, JUDGE, KING OR APOSTLE WHO WAS NOT AT TIMES BEWILDERED AS TO GOD'S INTENTION.

This type of questioning God is not uncommon for both Old or New Testament luminaries. With perhaps the exception of the Josephs and Daniels, it is hard to find a prophet, judge, king or apostle who was not at times bewildered as to God's intention. Since most of us have cried out, "God where are you? What's going on in my life?" we should never look down upon others when they are in this valley of despair.

Even the great prophet Elijah had his moments of vacillation, having just miraculously called down fire from Heaven and killed 450 prophets of Baal,.[67] (He was overcome with fear, hid in a cave, and wanted to die because King Ahab's wife Jezebel had vowed to kill him.) [68]

In the New Testament, it was no less than Jesus Himself who compared John the Baptist to Elijah, "And if you are willing to receive and accept it, John himself is Elijah who was to come *[before the kingdom]*."[69] Perhaps these two of history's greatest men had more similarities than some of us would like to acknowledge?

After establishing His credentials as a healer and deliverer in Luke 7, Jesus follows up with an extraordinarily revealing statement. He challenges John with, "And blessed is he who is not offended because of Me...."[70] Jesus is in essence saying, "Blessed is he who is not offended in the things I put him through." Another translation would be, "Happy and to be envied are those who refuse to question God in the hour of their greatest personal pain." Quite a statement! Certainly rich with implications, when spoken to a man who would soon have his head chopped off.

When King David was likewise facing death due to old age, his parting words give us a glimpse into his view of God's faithfulness during his remarkable life, "As the Lord lives, who has redeemed my life from every distress...."[71] Did God actually rescue David every time? David had conquered both the wrath of the Philistine giant Goliath and the treach-ery of the psychotic King Saul. Like Jesus, when betrayed by those closest to Him, David was given wisdom to overcome the bitterness of his wife Michal and the treachery of his son Absalom. Though David failed miserably at times as a husband and father, and was even guilty of the heinous crimes of murder and adultery, God redeemed every ugly situa-tion in David's life for His glory, saying, "I have found David, the son of Jesse, a man after My own heart, who will do all My will."[72]

JOURNEYING TO FREAKDOM

My detour into drugs that started in Europe eventually warped my final year in college. It transformed me from the straight-laced president of my University's most prestigious fraternity and vice president of the Student Union, into an embittered leader of the campus anti-war movement. My inner turmoil led me to spearhead the takeover of the University's Dean's office and be tear-gassed at the Washington Monument. Once fer-vently begging friends to stay clear of drugs, I now openly mocked those who refused to indulge. Like Gollum in the Lord of the Rings trilogy, my self-delusion into the world of drugs transformed me from a carefree life of the party, into a paranoid, lewd, and cynical recluse.

The final distortion in my college career came at graduation. Having used my God-given gift of persuasion to entice one of my psychology professors to give each of his students an A grade, he and I then smoked weed and jeered while watching the commencement ceremonies from an adjacent hillside. The words of Solomon, the overindulgent King of Israel, seem more than befitting for my tragic state of mind, "Therefore I hated life be-cause the work that was done under the sun was distressing to me, for all is vanity and grasping for the wind."[73]

Upon returning from England, I realized my obsession with the mystery girl had not diminished. Desperate to end the emotional fixation, I asked to speak with her. Once alone, I anxiously shared my heart. It was embarrassing, even pathetic, but necessary. I hoped at last the spell would be broken and I could move on with my life. She graciously listened, and at one point held my hand to console me. The conversation ended with me feeling like a complete idiot.

But, as the enemy of my soul would have it, within six months she and I were living together. Though the relationship seemed to begin in the heights of Heaven, it eventually ended in the caverns of hell. Within a few months, this supposed girl of my dreams told me she was pregnant. Though she begged me to marry her and raise the baby, I arrogantly insisted, "I don't believe in marriage. You need to get an abortion." A few days later, in September 1971, before abortions were legalized in the U.S., I drove her to a building in lower Manhattan and gave her $100 to vacuum away our child.

Overcome with shame, I couldn't even watch her walk into the building, nor was I willing to look at her when she returned. We drove away in silence. All of my sophisticated rationalizations couldn't gloss over what we had done. The pat justifications I would regularly chant, "It's not a baby! It's just tissue! It's the best choice!" seemed like the shallow, self-indulgent clichés they really were. None of those fabrications could dull the haunting reality; a part of me had died. I had killed my first child. It was the beginning of the end of our relationship.

I didn't find out until much later that, at the time of the abortion, our baby had a beating heart, breathing lungs, and brain waves. As the prophet Micah so candidly wrote, "I gave the fruit of my body for the sin of my soul."[74]

Once again, what I thought I wanted was the last thing I really needed. How much pointless pain would we each be spared if we could just surrender our will to God? It is only by trusting God that we can arrive at the safe, peaceful place He intended for us from the beginning.

PLUNDERING HELL... POPULATING HEAVEN

In the early 1980s, a couple who would later become dear friends of Suzie and mine, Trevor and Jan Yaxley, decided to take the plunge into full-time ministry. Trevor had been a successful businessman in New Zealand who had given his life fully to Jesus. He once prayed, "God, whatever you want to do in my life, go ahead." He and Jan were led by God to donate much of their own finances to the ministry, beginning an exhilarating faith venture that would have an enormous impact on their entire nation.

God had opened significant doors for Trevor and Jan's ministry and gave them great favor, even with New Zealand's political leaders. When a deadly typhoon ravaged islands in the South Pacific, Trevor organized a massive relief effort that moved the nation to reach out to those in need. For his efforts he was honored by the Prime Minister of New Zealand and emerged as one of the most respected Christian leaders in that nation.

In the early 1990s, my family—Suzie, our 12-year-old twin daughters and I—were invited by Trevor and Jan to minister throughout New Zealand. As our tour vans drove through the windy roads of this beautiful nation, I asked Trevor to share his life story with us, to perhaps get a glimpse as to why God was using him so mightily. We then had what was possibly the most memorable car ride of our lives.

Trevor shared that he and Jan were blessed with three children; the oldest was Mark, born with Down's Syndrome. David was next, followed by Becky, the youngest. Trevor and David shared an especially close relationship, becoming best friends. One stormy winter night a few years before, Trevor had been speaking in a nearby town on the North Island of New Zealand. As the meeting ended, he exhorted his son David, then 16, to drive home carefully as it was raining quite hard. David's 13-year-old sister Becky and a friend of hers accompanied him. Trevor and Jan left a half-hour later.

Making their way along the rain soaked road, Trevor and Jan came upon the flashing lights of ambulances and a helicopter overhead. Instantly, Trevor knew it was David. Coming over a hill, the shining lights of cars pointed downward into a ravine where their son's car lay mangled around a tree. Trevor jumped from his vehicle and proceeded to rush down the steep embankment. As he approached the shattered vehicle, an ambulance attendant grabbed his arm saying, "You can't go down there. There's a real mess underneath that blanket." Overwhelmed with grief, Trevor responded, "That mess is my son." The ambulance attendant was so shocked by the statement, Trevor had to pry the attendant's hand from his arm.

Running over to his son, Trevor lifted the blanket and embraced David. Sobbing uncontrollably, he then began to pray aloud, "God, I thank you for the 16 years you gave me with my precious son. Lord, I now give him back to you." An anonymous crowd gathered on the hillside and stood vigil in the rain. Quietly they listened to the cries of an anguished father. Trevor then felt led to invite anyone on the hillside to give his or her life to Jesus, and a number that night did.

Trevor and Jan's daughter, Becky, had been life-flighted to a nearby hospital. There, by her bedside, they sat vigil for many days despite having just lost a son. Sadly, Becky's friend had also been killed in the accident. Finally, a doctor gave them the grim news—Becky had a ten percent chance of making it through the night. Walking outside alone, exhausted and grief-stricken, Trevor looked up into the night sky and cried out, "Satan, you've taken my son from me, but you will not have my daughter! You've taken one son from me, but I'm going to spend the rest of my life taking thousands of sons and daughters from you."

There was a shift in the heavenly realms that night. Trevor and Jan had won the battle for Becky's life. Today, she is alive and well, married with children. Trevor also kept his promise. During the following years, he led thousands of New Zealanders to Jesus.

As Trevor shared his gut-wrenching life story with us, driving along in the van, we didn't just cry as a family, we sobbed. After he finished confiding in us one of the most difficult situations in his life, we fully understood why God had used his family so mightily.

A couple of years after her beloved son David died, Jan was fighting depression on a daily basis. Little did she know, her breakthrough was about to happen. One grief-stricken day, as she was working around her home listening to Christian music, a familiar song came on that struck her in an unusual way. "And David danced before the Lord with all his might." Right then Jan thought, "If my son David is dancing before the Lord with all of his might, what am I doing feeling sorry for myself down here?" Taking stock of her wounded soul she turned the music as loud as possible and began dancing around the room. The heaviness lifted as she envisioned dancing before the Lord with her son David. I trust they have been dancing together ever since.

God never tires of trying to form His eternal character in us. Responding poorly to life's greatest tests merely puts us back in line to wait for another opportunity to react with godly character. Responding well brings us face to face with the destiny for which we were created.

SOMETHING'S GOT TO GIVE

The abortion signaled the downfall of my connection with my college girlfriend. As the relationship declined so, too, did my fragile mental state. It seemed my every thought turned to suicide. I would spend days lying in bed, staring at the wall, overcome with self-pity, hating my life, and absolutely unable to dig my way out of my mental quagmire.

I was increasingly unstable. At the conclusion of college, my friends and I traveled across the country in a packed hippie van, intent on starting a commune in Mexico. But nothing I tried could keep my life from unraveling. Though we still traveled together, by that time the relationship with my girlfriend was completely over.

After being rejected by authorities at the Mexican border, our motley crew settled for the night on a remote Arizona road. In a deranged state of mind, I wandered aimlessly into the barren desert. Miserable and longing to die on that star-filled night, I took out a pocketknife and began to carve on my wrists. Fortunately, the knife was dull, and my mother's incessant prayers were sharp enough to pierce through the arrogance of my dis-illusioned heart.

Kneeling amongst the sagebrush, I screamed to the God I didn't believe in, "God help me!" Looking back on that fateful moment, there was so much deception in my life, I didn't even realize what I had said until many months later. But the prayer had been prayed, and the God who sees and hears everything responded to my cry.

By the time our magical, mystery tour landed in northern California a week later, I was threatening suicide constantly. No one knew what to do with me. Out of options, they put me alone on a plane bound for Hawaii. My twin brother Joseph, my best friend Bruce, and my ex-girlfriend were all there. This time, though, she aborted me—giving me $100, basically to get out of her life for good.

Be careful what you sow; it will come back to you. In fact, in one of his letters to a church, Paul warns "Do not be deceived, God is not mocked; for whatever a man sows, that he will also reap."[75] It is one of life's guarantees, for better or worse.

INTO THE GREAT WIDE OPEN

As the plane took off from Sacramento airport, like King Nebuchadnezzar in the Book of Daniel, I was "...driven from men..."[76]; completely stripped and emptied of all hope—utterly alone. As the early morning flight took off, the first golden rays of sunlight glistened in my tear-filled eyes. My desperate thought was, "I'm going to either meet God or die." Little did I know both would eventually come to pass.

Within a couple of months, I was reunited for a short time with my friend Bruce, who, like me, had also been disillusioned with religion. At one point, we knelt together on a remote beach on the Hawaiian Island of Molokai and earnestly prayed, "Jesus, Krishna, Buddha, we can see from reading your teachings that you are not the same person. Would you please reveal yourself to us?"

Three months later, upon returning to the Sacramento area, I went to visit Bruce and his mother on Mother's Day, 1972. At that time, I had been traveling with a woman from the planet Venus. We were on a mission to Lake Titicaca in Peru to rendezvous with agents from an interplanetary government known as "Xion." (Sounds reasonable, doesn't it?)

After listening to my exotic adventures, I asked Bruce what was going on in his life. He told me, "Jesus!" I said, "Jesus is great! He's a great prophet; a great teacher!" Bruce retorted, "No, Francis, just Jesus!" I thought, "How narrow! What can you do with just Jesus?"

Bruce shared how he had returned from Hawaii, determined to find God. Going into a remote wooded area, his search for the divine led to endlessly chanting prayers to Krishna every day for a full month. Instead of reaching enlightenment, however, his efforts only brought him close to a nervous breakdown.

Returning in desperation to his hometown of Marysville, Bruce walked into the Episcopal Church he had grown up in. It was mid-day and no one was around. Barefoot and wearing a saffron robe, he went to the front of the sanctuary, where he knelt before a statue of Jesus hanging on a cross. Collapsing in an emotional heap, he prayed an anguished, sobbing prayer, "I don't know much about You, except what I heard here as a young boy growing up. But, if You can, please help me." At that moment, he was knocked backward and all of the pressures plaguing his troubled mind were instantly lifted. Every question he had was either answered or suddenly seemed insignificant.

PERFECT TIMING
As Bruce shared with me how his life had been transformed, I was captivated. Here was a credible person, who had, like me, been desperately searching for meaning in his life.

That night we drove into the Sierra foothills, to a little country church in Smartsville, California. The genuineness of the guest speaker gripped my searching soul. A former hippie himself, he sang and authentically shared how Jesus had transformed his own life. His humility was irrefutable!

During the previous season of my life in Hawaii, I had experienced firsthand the mystical lure of Eastern religions while chanting for hours in Krishna temples. Now, in this remote country church I prayed under my breath, "Jesus, I don't know if you are who this man says you are, but if you are, do for me what you did for him."

It wasn't a passive, indifferent prayer. God knew my past all too well. He had witnessed each misguided attempt to satisfy the emptiness inside. Now, upon finally accepting Jesus Christ as my Lord and Savior, I had an extraordinary physiological experience. After praying this simple prayer, I began to be choked by the necklaces I was wearing—a set of Japa Beads, used to chant to Krishna, and a turquoise necklace, which I believed communicated to Venusians (people from Venus).

Unable to breathe or move my hands to help, I then prayed the second prayer, "Jesus help me!" Instantly, my hands were free to move. I reached up and ripped the necklaces off. Hundreds of beads scattered all over the floor and I could breathe once again.

As I cried for some time, people began to gather around me and explain why I had been so dramatically impacted. At the point I had invited Jesus Christ to come and live in my spirit, a battle transpired. Crying out to the one true God I didn't know, the former gods (actually demons) I had previously worshipped, had once and for all been removed from my life. I had been born again! For the next month, I was so high on God I thought I would never come down. Eventually, I learned that even though God had used a strong physical experience to capture and liberate my heart, my relationship with God was intended to be a walk of faith not feelings.

I was born again on Mother's Day, May 14, 1972. From the beginning I knew it was because of my mother's prayers. During my college years, my precious mother had endured such grief, particularly from me. At times, when she would reverentially bow her head to pray over her food, I would laugh aloud in her face. I will be forever indebted to her for her love, prayers and perseverance. Though I had not seen her since leaving New York City nine months prior, she had been fervently interceding for my reckless life. Many years later, when I happened upon my boyhood Catholic missal (prayerbook), I also realized May 14ᵀᴴ was the same day I had received my First Holy Communion some 15 years earlier. Truly the Lord knows each of the days of our lives.[77]

JESUS NEVER INTENDED TO KILL ME PHYSICALLY, BUT HIS PERFECT SCRIPT FOR MY LIFE ALWAYS INCLUDED MY LEARNING TO DIE TO MYSELF.

Having been given my mother's name—Frances—I was the first of her five children to receive the Lord. Today, all of my siblings are continuing in their deeply personal relationships with Jesus. Their intimacy with God now spans more than 30 years. Our mother truly prayed each of us into the Kingdom of God. A devout Roman Catholic, this little Italian lady, early on, realized the power of prayer. [78]

Part one of my fleeting thought on the lonely flight from Sacramento to Hawaii had been answered. I had determined that I was going to either meet God or die. I had truly found God! Now, part two was about to be resolved as well; just not in the way I expected. Jesus never intended to kill me physically, but His perfect script for my life always included my learning to die to myself. As it says in 2 Corinthians 5:17, "Therefore, if anyone is in Christ, he is a new creation; old things have passed away; behold, all things have become new."

DEAD PEOPLE DON'T WHINE

So, how should we respond to the greatest difficulties in life? There's one sure-fire way. David wrote part of his secret in the Psalms, "The Lord says, 'Be still and know that I am God.' "[79] When are we most still? When we are sleeping? No. Videotape replays reveal most people toss and turn.

All of us are most still when we are dead. Try to irritate a dead person and he won't even look at you; jump on his head—again, complete indifference. Temptations mean nothing to him, nor does any amount of peer pressure. Why? Because he is dead—dead to fear, dead to worry, dead to anger, dead to lust—he is beyond the seductions of this earth. You could paraphrase Psalm 46:10, "Drop dead and know that I am God."

All of us want resurrection life, but we will never have it until we are dead. (How can one be resurrected if he is not dead?) Paul never said, "I die monthly—when the bills come in... I die yearly—during tax season." No, he proclaimed, "...I die daily."[80] He said, "I'm a dead man, walking!"

How often should we die to ourselves—our own ambitions and self-will? Resurrection life is only available to dead people. If Jesus had to die to get it, so do we. But His promise to us is sure: "...if the Spirit of Him who raised Jesus from the dead dwells in you, He who raised Christ from the dead will also give life to your mortal bodies through His Spirit who dwells in you."[81] How can you tell if you are dead? When you are asleep in a boat in the middle of a storm. When someone slaps you on one cheek, and you turn the other one. When all hell is breaking loose and you are at total peace. Dead men don't whine!

Paul proclaimed triumphantly, "But what things were gain to me, these I have counted loss for Christ. Yet indeed I also count all things loss for the excellence of the knowledge of Christ Jesus my Lord, for whom I have suffered the loss of all things, and count them as rubbish *[Greek—dung, garbage]*, that I may gain Christ... that I may know Him and the power of His resurrection, and the fellowship of His sufferings, being conformed to His death, if, by any means, I may attain to the resurrection from the dead."[82]

Wow! Paul considered even the greatest things he could gain in life as "garbage and dung" compared to having an intimate relationship with the Lord Jesus Christ. These things were the premiere dimensions of his life: loved ones, hopes and dreams, possessions and ambitions. Compared to knowing Jesus they were all "dung."

The *World English Dictionary* defines *dung* as "the solid excrement of animals." I don't know about you, but I've never been a big fan of animal waste. Yet, Paul candidly shared that having the resurrection life Jesus offered made everything else seem like garbage in comparison.

SUMMARY POINTS

- Responding well brings us face to face with the destiny for which we were created.

- My contentment has nothing to do with what is happening around me, and everything to do with what is happening inside me.

QUESTIONS FOR DISCUSSION

1. What does contentment mean to you? What impacts your contentment?

2. Think of a time when you blamed others and God when circumstances didn't work out the way you thought they should. How long were you stuck in blame? In what ways did you respond? How did that affect your relationships with God and others?

3. Romans 8:28 says, "For we know that all things work together for the good of those who love God, who walk according to His purposes." What does this promise of God personally say to you? What are the areas of your life where you don't act as if this promise is true? Explain.

4. What breakthrough do you currently need in your life? How do you think you'll respond if that breakthrough doesn't come?

5. In what ways do you live out "dying to self" in your daily life? How does that impact your life?

CHAPTER FIVE

JESUS, PLUS NOTHING, IS EVERYTHING

BORN AND RAISED IN SMARTSVILLE

Smartsville, California is located right next door to the northern California gold rush towns of Timbuctoo and Rough and Ready. In the early 1970s, it had a booming population of 200. It was there in late 1971, six months prior to my arrival, that a band of newly converted hippies purchased the rundown Smartsville Hotel and other adjacent buildings. A Christian community, called Morning Star Ranch, was born.

Throughout the early and mid-70s, hundreds of nomadic young people like myself passed through Smartsville, got saved, and plugged into life as Jesus Freaks. At the height of this mini-revival, it was common for us to baptize ten–15 people every Sunday. After church, we would jump in our battered pick-up trucks and head down a dusty road to Timbuctoo. While singing songs about Jesus, fellow converts were fully immersed in the chilly waters of the Yuba River—before God, angels, demons, friends and curious sunbathers.

Our one-room Smartsville Community Church could only seat 100 people, but during the summer of 1973 hungry believers would pack in, wall to wall. Desperate to hear about God, some would even stand in the miniature lobby or crowd outside the building. With a tin roof, no air conditioning, and the 100+ degree heat of a California summer, the building was stifling during our two-to-three-hour long meetings. At times sweat would drip down my legs, soaking my shoes.

Having been radically saved in this youth revival, even today, the desire of my heart is to once again see waves of young people transformed by Jesus Christ. I spend many fruitful hours each week being a surrogate father to dozens of 15-to-25-year-olds in the hopes that they, too, will turn their generation upside down.

The scripture, "Train up a child in the way he should go, and when he is old he will not depart from it"[83] applies here. Every phase of our lives, even during our spiritual infancy, is preparation for the eventual stewardships God will give us as we mature.

REMOVING THE STING OF DEATH

As a baby Christian, I remember repeatedly hearing about the work Jesus accomplished on the cross. At times, I would get annoyed when people talked about the cross as if it was the panacea for whatever ails you. Little did I know, it was. One of the first songs I wrote after receiving Jesus said, "I had some thoughts of God before I met Him. Yes, He even seemed to look a lot like me. But when I saw the cross of my Savior, I knew I was as blind as I could be." No longer did simplicity seem too simple. On the contrary, my uncomplicated relationship with Jesus had become the most refreshing experience of my entire life.

For far too long I had done whatever my heart desired. As a Christian, I quickly settled into living for God's will and not my own. It has been said, "We don't know what will bring the most glory to God, our life or our death." Not only is this true for each of our lives, it was first true in Jesus' life. "He was willing to die a shameful death on the cross because of the joy He knew would be His afterward."[84] We each need to realize that there is joy in the cross, not just for Jesus, but for ourselves as well.

I once read a short newspaper article about a couple in North Carolina. Jerry and Dolores Burdette were newly married and had everything to live for. One day, as they walked along a beach, they heard cries for help coming from the churning surf. Three people were drowning. The first had been helplessly captured by the undertow; one by one each of the others had entered the water to help, only to be sucked into the undertow as well. All three were fighting for their lives.

As soon as Jerry saw their predicament, he dove in as well. An excellent swimmer, Jerry reached the closest person and brought him safely to shore. He then dove back in and rescued the second. Completely exhausted, but seeing the plight of the third drowning soul, Jerry, without regard for his own safety, swam back out and grabbed hold of the last person. Though Jerry was able to get the final victim close enough to shore to make it back on his own, he himself was so depleted of strength he was unable to continue. Jerry sank out of sight as his precious bride watched, having given his life for three complete strangers.

I have often thought of that brave, faceless man and wondered what happened to his wife Dolores and those three people Jerry died for. What responsibility had any of the three taken for Dolores' well-being? They were drowning in a violent ocean and a passerby gave his life to rescue them. As each one crawled onto the shore and greeted his wife, I can't imagine they would walk away having only thanked her half-heartedly. Her husband had died to save each of them, and in doing so her life was forever changed. Her well-being should, in some way, be their responsibility because the one she lived for had given his life for them. I have prayed for Dolores on a number of occasions that her life would be doubly blessed. She had married a noble man, who selflessly gave his life for others.

We see this same principle in the life of Jesus. All of us were drowning in an ocean of sin, incapable of saving ourselves, when the God of the Universe—the one we had each rejected by countless selfish acts— willingly sacrificed Himself for us. He died on a cross in the most brutal way imaginable just so we might live with Him forever. How grateful should we be to such a God, for such a selfless action? Spending eternity thanking and praising Him would still pale in comparison to what He gave for each of us. Jesus underscored the cost of love when he said, "Greater love has no one than this, than to lay down one's life for his friends."[85]

On the other hand, if you were short one penny and the sales person said, "Go ahead, take a penny," would your eyes well up with tears for his generosity? Would you then say, "I will never forget you for as long as I live!" No, it was just a penny. To the extent we have been rescued, that is the extent we should be grateful.

In the Gospel of Luke, an immoral woman came to a house where Jesus was staying and, kneeling beside Jesus, weeping, washed His dirty feet with her tears. As those around her looked on in astonishment, she wiped His feet with her hair, continually kissing and anointing them with expensive perfume. Seeing this shocking display of affection, one hypocritical Pharisee spoke to himself, saying, "This Man, if He were a prophet, would know who and what manner of woman this is who is touching Him, for she is a sinner.'"[86] Jesus, however, knew his thoughts and replied, "...her sins, which are many, are forgiven, for she loved much. But to whom little is forgiven, the same loves little."[87]

Being a little sinner is like being a little pregnant—you either are or you're not. If you are forgiven, then you're completely forgiven. If we are truly forgiven we should be as grateful as a person who has just been rescued from a horrible death.

Paul the Apostle clearly understood this revelation. Though once a persecutor of Christians, his radical conversion left him an enthusiastic follower of Jesus Christ. When Paul wrote, "...so now also Christ will be magnified in my body, whether by life or by death. For to me, to live is Christ, and to die is gain."[88] He was, in essence, saying that there are two marvelous options for each of us: life or death. Both are tremendous choices if our lives truly belong to the God of the Universe.

IF WE ARE TRULY FORGIVEN WE SHOULD BE AS GRATEFUL AS A PERSON WHO HAS JUST BEEN RESCUED FROM A HORRIBLE DEATH.

THE BRIDE OF MY YOUTH

In the spring of 1974, two years after my conversion, I volunteered to help plant a church in South Lake Tahoe, California. It was there I fell head-over-heels in love with my beautiful wife, Suzie.

Suzie's first marriage had been to her high school sweetheart. After she became a Christian, she prayed for him to receive Jesus, but to no avail. Tragically, on the day he was going to file for divorce, he was killed flying a single-engine plane.

At the time of the crash, Suzie was living in the Sister's Dorm at Morning Star Ranch. Around midnight on the day of his fatal accident, her dad and mom came to break the news to her. Sobbing quietly, she went into her dorm room to pack some clothes. A scripture on the wall above the bed caught her eye. It was a New Testament verse that would become pivotal, not just for Suzie's life, but for mine as well. Romans 8:28 says, "And we know that God causes everything to work together for the good of those who love God and are called according to His purpose for them."

As the truth of this hope-filled scripture entered her heart, a calming peace gave her an inner confidence God had everything under control. Within six months, she had joined our church planting team in Lake Tahoe, and a short while later we fell in love. God had brought both of our dysfunctional lives full circle.

Suzie and I were married on November 1, 1975, in one of Morning Star's refurbished buildings. This former antique shop, post office, and bank had even at one time been a jail. How appropriate for two former spiritual outlaws! Both Suzie and I, having had our share of near-death experiences, are now committed to never giving up on anyone; firmly believing every life is redeemable.

Now, over three decades later, we have spent our lives giving hope to the hopeless; loving the seemingly unlovable, and watching God restore thousands of broken lives. Only by allowing God to heal us, can we realize our true destiny: helping others get healed in the same areas God has healed us.

JESUS, PLUS NOTHING, IS EVERYTHING

In Chapter One, I wrote about a challenging season when it seemed many of the Christian projects I was working on did not work out. All of my efforts were coming up empty. God's supernatural blessing, which at one point was evident in my life on a daily basis, was suddenly turned off. Doors were slamming shut and not reopening. I kept waiting for something to change. It wasn't a passing season; it was God making a solemn statement. He was rebooting my life.

One night, in the midst of my turmoil, I went on a sovereign prayer walk with God. As I looked into the starry sky I prayed from the deepest part of my being, "Jesus, even if I lose everything, I can't lose You." It wasn't a cry of despair, it was a confident acknowledgment of God's unshakeable hand on my life. Deep inside, I knew nothing could

separate me from God's love and care. My absolute conviction was, even if I lost everything else, His love for me would remain unshakeable.

This prayer was a major epiphany, spawning the life-changing revelation, "Jesus, Plus
Nothing, Is Everything." God, and nothing else, is all I need. He alone is committed to
my good, no matter what happens. Nothing but Jesus is important; everything could be
stripped from my life, and I will still be sustained. I was exhausted from trying to see
the projects completed; the above prayer of resignation produced a massive release of
pressure. I didn't have to make things work out. My heart was being changed to enjoy
the process of just knowing Him.

THE SECRET OF SATISFACTION

For years I have asked audiences, "Who here has not had a very difficult life? Please
stand; we want to beat you up." Obviously, no hands are raised. It's true; life is hard.
Yet, finding fulfillment in God is His will for each of us.

If anyone knew how to find satisfaction in life, it was the person God considered "a man
after [His] own heart"—King David. David once wrote, "I will be satisfied when I awake in
Your likeness."[89] David wasn't saying, "I will be satisfied when I go to Heaven" or "I will
be satisfied when all of my problems work out." Instead he responded out of the realization that God is the only One who will ever satisfy.

If the police came to your home with a search warrant and you told them they could check
anywhere except a certain closet, that would become the first place they would look. In
the same way, God is more concerned with the parts of our hearts that we haven't surrendered to Him than with the parts we have. Therefore, He doesn't give us what we think we
need; God changes our hearts so that we value what He alone knows we really need.

So, how are we changed into God's likeness? Jesus tells us plainly, "Most assuredly, I say
to you, unless a grain of wheat falls into the ground and dies, it remains alone; but if it
dies, it produces much grain. He who loves his life will lose it, and he who hates his life in
this world will keep it for eternal life."[90] The only way to find satisfaction in life is to die to
our agenda and surrender to God's. It is in dying we live. "For you died when Christ died,
and your real life is hidden with Christ in God."[91]

HEAVEN INCREASES AND EARTH RECEDES

Paul the Apostle understood very well the principle of Jesus being everything. He emphatically wrote in to Colossians 3, "If then you were raised with Christ, seek those things which are above, where Christ is, sitting at the right hand of God. Set your mind [affections] on things above, not on things on the earth. For you died, and your life is hidden with Christ in God."[92]

When I was a young Christian, I was driving with a seasoned missionary in an Asian nation. We had come to a stoplight, where two lanes merged into one. In the next lane, revving his engine, was a young guy in a brand new sports car. When the light turned green, much to my horror, the missionary floored the accelerator and cut off the sports car. All the while yelling, "No one gets ahead of the man of God!" I was speechless. I could not believe that this man of God really thought being first was actually the goal in life.

On the contrary, if we elbow our way to the front of the line eventually we will come face to face with Christ's fine print, "But many who are first will be last, and the last first."[93] I don't have to push my weight around; I just have to follow Jesus. In the end, He's the only One worth following anyway.

WHY ARE YOU HANGING AROUND?

Most people hung around Jesus for the loaves and the fishes—the proverbial hot meals. But His true disciples were completely committed even to the point of death. Trying to shake loose the sheep from the goats, Jesus once taught, "I assure you, unless you eat the flesh of the Son of Man and drink his blood, you cannot have eternal life within you."[94]

Jesus clearly did not make the bar as low as possible. Instead, the truth is quite the opposite: the only relationship Jesus is willing to have with anyone is a high-commitment relationship; the same kind a spouse requires. No spouse ever hoped his or her mate would be unfaithful. We each expect, even demand, 100 percent faithfulness. There are no allowances for affairs, not even on our birthdays. Jesus asks for no less commitment—no less devotion.

Jesus set the bar even higher when he said, "But those who eat my flesh and drink my blood have eternal life, and I will raise them at the last day. For my flesh is the true food, and my blood is the true drink. All who eat my flesh and drink my blood remain in Me, and I in them."[95]

This hardly sounds reasonable. In fact, it was a little offensive. Even His disciples complained to each other, "This is very hard to understand. How can anyone accept it?" Yet Jesus knew that His disciples were confused, so He asked them, "Does this offend you?"[96] But His metaphor made the point. He was insistent: follow Me completely, or don't follow Me at all! "At this point many of His disciples turned away and deserted Him."[97] Yet, contrary to popular opinion, dying to self is not a miserable experience. It is designed by God to be one of the most exhilarating adventures in life.

DYING GRACEFULLY

A hundred years ago, a passenger ship sank while crossing the Atlantic Ocean. As it was going down, the occupants realized there were not enough lifeboats or life jackets for everyone on board. Word spread quickly, soon coming to the attention of 109 Salvation Army officers. Consulting together, they made a courageous decision. They would each give their life jackets to others on board.

After the ship sank, and the bodies of all 109 Salvation Army officers were found—not one of them had on a life jacket. They had each drowned, willingly giving their lives for total strangers. Numerous reports of the officers' heroism were shared among the survivors. Over and over again, survivor's reported how the Salvation Army officers took off their own life jackets for others. Many of them, even women, persuading full-grown men to put on the jackets, pleading, "Take the jacket! I can die better than you can."

Could we make the same offer to those around us today? The struggle is we all want a life jacket. Nobody wants to die. Out of everyone on earth, Christians should be the ones who best know how to die; dying daily to our own desires and wants.

OUT OF EVERYONE ON EARTH, CHRISTIANS SHOULD BE THE ONES WHO BEST KNOW HOW TO DIE; DYING DAILY TO OUR OWN DESIRES AND WANTS.

If we do not have a heart to reach out to other people, we will eventually spend our lives chasing after lesser things. Fervent, dedicated people will always be consumed by something related to God. Yet, there seem to be many genuinely sincere Christians who are unwilling or unable to reach out to a lost and dying world.

Some have spent their lives in mental speculation, tantalized by theological or eschatological possibilities. Yes, first love the Lord your God with all of your heart, mind, soul and strength; and out of that head-over-heels love relationship with God, we must love our neighbor as much as we love ourselves. Love should be the foundation of everything in our lives. Paul wrote, "If I gave everything I have to the poor and even sacrificed my body, I could boast about it; but if I didn't love others, I would be of no value whatsoever."[98]

If the net effect of loving God is merely to muse on how much He loves us, then somehow we have not heard His heart in His presence. The God who once loved the world, still does. He continually invites us, those who have truly been washed, healed, touched and refreshed in His presence, to leave the comforts of Heaven and join Him in the battle for Earth.

As Oswald Chambers so eloquently said, "We are not made for brilliant moments, but we have to walk in the light of them in ordinary ways. There was only one brilliant moment in the life of Jesus, and that was on the Mount of Transfiguration; then He emptied Himself the second time of His glory, and came down into the demon-possessed valley. For 33 years Jesus laid out His life to do the will of His Father...."[99]

Jesus was dead long before He went to the cross; not dead physically, but dead to sin—dead to His own will! If we really want to be like Jesus, we must first understand who He really was. He was a man of sorrows and acquainted with grief; despised and rejected, bruised, oppressed and afflicted.[100] Just like us, Jesus spent His whole life learning how to die to Himself and live for the Father and a lost and dying world.

DYING PERFECTLY

Only one person ever perfectly modeled dying: the Lord Jesus Christ. In the Gospel of Mark, Jesus, nearing the end of His earthly ministry, came to the Garden of Gethsemane. Knowing the great battle He was about to face, "He said to His disciples, 'Sit here while I pray.' And He then took Peter, James, and John with Him, and began to be troubled and deeply distressed. Then Jesus said to them, 'My soul is exceedingly sorrowful, even to death. Stay here and watch.' "[101]

Jesus wasn't exaggerating the extent of His trouble, distress and sorrow! He was literally about to become the sin of the world. Consumed in grief, He felt like dying. This must have been the worst nightmare of His life. "He went a little farther, and fell on the ground, and prayed that if it were possible, the hour might pass from Him. And He said, 'Abba, Father, all things are possible for You. Take this cup away from Me; nevertheless, not what I will, but what You will.' "[102]

Jesus had spent His whole life disciplining His soul to die. Therefore, His response in the Garden of Gethsemane had three appropriate dimensions: complete faith, a willingness to forsake His own personal preference, and absolute trust.

First, Jesus had complete faith in the will of His Heavenly Father. He prayed unequivocally, "All things are possible for You." No solution was outside the reach of His Father in Heaven.

Secondly, Jesus expressed His human response to a heavenly dilemma, "Take this cup away from Me." What was this cup He preferred to not drink? The pain of crucifixion? Dying early in life? Leaving those He loved? I do not believe Jesus was unwilling to embrace any of the human challenges He faced. "...Christ Jesus came into the world to save sinners...."[103]

His challenge lay in eternity. When Jesus became sin for all humankind,[104] at that moment His fellowship with His Father was broken. "God is light and in Him is no darkness at all."[105] The God of light could have "...no fellowship with the unfruitful works of darkness...."[106] On this side of eternity, we can have no idea how excruciatingly painful breaking fellowship with His Father was for the Lord Jesus Christ. Yet, without hesitation, Jesus was willing to temporarily lay aside His perfect bond with His Father in order to restore our relationship with God.

Summoning an inner strength, and resting on an absolute trust in God the Father, Jesus immediately yielded His will to the third and final appropriate response saying, "Nevertheless, not what I will, but what You will." What a perfect blend of faith and trust! What a perfect example for each of us!

LIVING BEYOND PERSONAL PREFERENCE
In the Book of Acts, Paul the Apostle faced the greatest challenge of his life: death by

beheading. A prophetic word predicted going to Jerusalem meant danger, imprisonment and ultimately death. Paul likewise exhibited complete faith, a forsaking of his own personal preference, and absolute trust. He acknowledged, "And see, now I go bound in the spirit to Jerusalem, not knowing the things that will happen to me there, except that the Holy Spirit testifies in every city, saying that chains and tribulations await me."[107]

Paul refused to cower in fear at the likelihood of his suffering and death. Instead, he shot back, "But none of these things move me; nor do I count my life dear to myself, so that I may finish my race with joy, and the ministry which I received from the Lord Jesus, to testify to the gospel of the grace of God."[108] Paul again demonstrates complete faith and absolute trust in God. Is it any wonder Paul was chosen to write so much of the New Testament?

If we give into fear and personal preference, each of us will misinterpret the most important decisions of our lifetime. Likewise, if we are more concerned with preserving our lives, we will fail to fulfill God's perfect will for us. The breakthrough perspective each of us need most is, "Nothing is going to shake me!" You know you are dead when nothing can shake your dependence upon God. Sooner or later we each need to accept this fact: God is NOT trying to change our circumstances, He's trying to change our reaction to our circumstances.

I attempt to live every day beyond my addiction to having my own way. I consciously choose to trust the God I know, to fully discern the things I don't. He alone has all past, present and future understanding at His disposal, in order to make the decisions that are truly in my best interest. For only in eternity will I fully realize how God perfectly orchestrated every dimension of my life.

GOD IS NOT TRYING TO CHANGE OUR CIRCUMSTANCES, HE'S TRYING TO CHANGE OUR REACTION TO OUR CIRCUMSTANCES.

My overpowering preference in life is to fully embrace God's preference. In anticipation of this, every day, I wake up excited to see what He has picked out for me. Having had a natural father who never planned anything special for my life, I now live continually in anticipation of the magnificent surprises my heavenly Father has prepared for me. "No eye has seen, no ear has heard, and no mind has imagined what God has prepared for those who love Him. But we know these things because God has revealed them to us by His Spirit...."[109]

DODGING DEATH AND LIVING LIFE

I knew a woman who was driving with her boyfriend in an open jeep. They were off-road, driving up a mountain in the Rockies, outside of Denver, Colorado. Her two daughters, five and seven years old, were both seat-belted in the back of the jeep.

As the boyfriend parked the vehicle on the side of a steep hill, he failed to set the brake properly. Moments after walking away, the jeep began to roll backwards down the hill, tumbling over and over while careening toward a cliff. Amazingly, because of their seat-belts, the girls were not thrown out.

The only thing that could keep the vehicle and the girls from launching over the cliff was one straggly tree perched at the edge of the precipice. If the jeep did not hit the tree perfectly, or if the tree failed to stop the jeep on impact, then the jeep and the two little girls would plummet over the cliff, falling to their death. But as God would have it, the tree caught the jeep, saving the girls' lives. Though the vehicle was totaled, the daughters walked away without a scratch.

I've thought a lot about that tree over the years. Many people would have considered the tree useless; sitting in the middle of nowhere, doing absolutely nothing of consequence. But God had a different plan. In His infinite wisdom He knew, "I'll make this tree, that no one will think has value, for one shining moment—to save two little girls."

I can also imagine as the tree sized up the situation, it braced for its big opportunity. At first, it had been spacing out in the afternoon sun, but seeing the jeep hurdling toward it, adrenalin shot through its trunk. Digging its roots in, bracing for impact, the tree gave everything it had to absorb the collision of the jeep; and much to its delight the children were spared.

That night, after the jubilant family had gone home, with the jeep permanently lodged in its wounded side, the bruised and battered tree probably called out to a friend on a nearby mountaintop, "Hey Aspen, did you see that today? You know how I'm always complaining about nothing significant ever happening to me? Well, today was different! This was the greatest day of my life! Today, I rescued two little girls from certain death. It made all those boring, lonely years worth living. For the rest of my life, I'll probably never have another opportunity like this, so I'll cherish this day forever."

Each of us at some point in our lives will find ourselves plummeting toward a cliff and certain death. In that moment, the only thing separating us from an eternity estranged from our loving Creator will be one straggly tree: the cross of Jesus. From the beginning of time that lone tree was in the heart of the Father, created for one purpose: to sacrifice His only Son for the sins of the world. If we miss that tree, our fate is sealed. If we embrace it, we will be eternally grateful that God spared our lives.

Whether we fully embrace it or not: Jesus, plus nothing, is everything. That fact is unalterable! He is the loving Bridegroom our hearts yearn for; the One we were created to spend eternity with. Ultimately, the choice is ours: we can accept Him now, or bow before Him later.

SUMMARY POINTS

- To the extent we have been rescued, that is the extent we should be grateful.

- Being a little sinner is like being a little pregnant—you either are or you're not.

- Nothing but Jesus is important; everything could be stripped from my life, and I will still be sustained.

- God doesn't give us what we think we need, He changes our hearts so that we value what He alone knows we really need.

- If we give in to fear and personal preference, each of us will misinterpret the most important decisions of our lifetime.

- God is NOT trying to change our circumstances, He's trying to change our reaction to our circumstances.

QUESTIONS FOR DISCUSSION

1. What do you fill your life with instead of Jesus? When are you most vulnerable to those other influences? How do they make you feel?

2. Now that you have identified the idols in your life, what is the short-term benefit to you having them? What is the long-term drawback?

3. What has God asked you to give up that you are struggling with? Why does that thing have so much value to you? What do you think will happen if you do give it up?

4. Who's preferences govern your life more often- God's or your own? In the past month, how have you chosen to "die" to your personal preferences? What impact did that have on your life?

5. What has been most challenging for you in this chapter? Why?

CHAPTER SIX

LIVING THE
TRANSPARENT LIFE

A transformed life is irrefutable.

FREE LOVE BANKRUPTED ME

Being a charter member in the free love movement cost so much, I'm still making payments. For years I tried to make love a god when, in truth, God is love. It was not until I found Jesus at 23 that I realized each of my many imperfections had been marvelously covered by God's matchless love and perfection.

I needed a Savior. He wanted a son.

We were made for each other.

Actually, I was made for Him.

For me, after my salvation, the summer of '72 was marked by 100-degree sweltering nights, endless oatmeal breakfasts, meatless lentil burgers, and venison Bumper Burgers (roadkill donated by the Fish and Game Department). In spite of what we didn't have, God's presence at Morning Star Ranch permeated our every waking moment. We were in love. We sang, laughed, and cried for joy. We wanted everyone in the world to know our Jesus and set out to tell anyone who would listen.

IT TAKES EXTRAORDINARY COURAGE AND AN ABSOLUTE WILLINGNESS TO LAY OUR LIVES BARE BEFORE OTHERS.

Though my longing for purpose was greatly satisfied when I was born again, my heart yearned to be fully immersed in a community of authentic people. My hope in knowing Jesus was that honesty with others would bring the complete overhaul I desperately needed. Initially it did, but the price for being fully transparent was difficult to maintain. Jesus summed up the challenge, "...he who does not gather with Me scatters."[110] Eventually my heart began to scatter.

Over time, my abject abandon turned into cautious commitment. The mantra, "I'll do anything for you, Jesus" morphed into "Now God, what exactly did You have in mind?" My willingness to do "whatever... for whomever... whenever" evolved into doing "somewhat... for some... sometimes." But the seed for an authentic relationship with my Creator had been firmly planted in my spirit. No substitute would do.

BREAKING THE SILENCE

John the Beloved, the disciple who perhaps best knew how much God loved him, once wrote, "This is the message which we have heard from Him and declare to you, that God is light and in Him is no darkness at all. If we say that we have fellowship with Him, and walk in darkness, we lie and do not practice the truth. But if we walk in the light as He is in the light, we have fellowship with one another, and the blood of Jesus Christ His Son cleanses us from all sin."[111]

"Walk in the light." What does that really mean? The original Greek text could be translated, "to make known one's thoughts, to be transparent, to break the silence." What an incredible concept! Many years ago, when I first began ministry, the vast majority of leaders I had were those who ministered out of their successes. I knew in my own life I had difficulty relating to a person who seemed to be victorious most of the time, when I found myself struggling so much to be like Jesus. So, while speaking to audiences, I began to open up and candidly tell of my own mistakes and struggles. To my surprise, the overwhelming response was positive. People liked my honesty and transparency more than any other part of my message! It was risky; it still is. It takes extraordinary courage and an absolute willingness to lay our lives bare before others. The Scriptures clearly teach we were created to share what is most precious *in* us, with those most precious *to* us. Only then are we walking in the light God intended.

Since 1997, my wife Suzie and I have had over 450 people in our home attending Leadership Groups. During our sessions, we have spent many hours sharing this one question: The areas in my life I am most concerned will hinder me from fulfilling God's will are

_____.

At the beginning of each new group, Suzie and I prime the pump by sharing the parts of our own lives that could potentially hinder us from fulfilling God's will in us. We have found that this one question goes deep into revealing the areas of possible vulnerability in each person's life. It breaks down the potential to be unreal and hide behind a superficial spiritual façade.

Over the many years we have been facilitating these spirit-opening and soul-baring sessions, we have been amazed at the candor and humility demonstrated by God's people. They each have something profound to share about who they are and what God has done in their lives. It is also imperative we understand where the soft underbelly of our weakness is. Paul the Apostle admonished all generations to remain acutely aware of our vulnerabilities, "...lest Satan should take advantage of us; for we are not ignorant of his devices."[112]

During one Leadership Group many years ago, a former pastor and his wife were invited to participate. He had been a senior pastor for seven years, and had experienced a great deal of hurt in his previous ministry. As the monthly meetings progressed, each person shared his or her issues.

During our last session, the former pastor and his wife were now the only remaining ones to share their lives. The wife went first. She shared vulnerably, opening her wounded heart to a group of friends who, having each shared their own frailties, were already sensitive to the delicate nuances of her life experience. All had gone well, and another group was once again headed for a safe, fulfilling landing.

Now, it was her husband's turn. If anyone in the room had been unaware of some of their pain from pastoring, her time of sharing had brought further understanding. The room was poised with compassion, and all of us were eager to encourage our wounded brother. Yet, what happened next still bothers me, even though several years have passed.

He looked around the room at each of us with a hardened, distant look on his face, before saying, "Frankly, I don't think I know any of you well enough. I don't feel comfortable sharing about my life with you." He then abruptly stopped speaking and just sat there.

You could have heard a pin drop. Instant whiplash! None of us wanted to put words in his mouth. All we were asking for, and I firmly believe the Spirit of God was hoping for, was for him to in some way share his life with others. But all he communicated with us was a glazed stare. He straight-armed the entire room. It was one of the saddest things I have ever witnessed. There was a moment, had he been honest in this place of safety, that he perhaps could have received a divine healing.

Much younger believers sat in stunned silence, astonished at what just transpired. The once safe and relaxed atmosphere had suddenly chilled. In a moment I understood why he was no longer a pastor. No one wants to follow a hardened, distant leader. Those of us who have followed them still bear the scars from their lack of honesty and forthrightness. It was devastating to watch this former pastor who had been so trained by poor examples to not expose his deep insecurities. Even when in a safe environment, he was unable to allow anyone else to identify with his pain. Once again, hurt people hurt people.

The words of Jesus sound even more transparent with this perspective in mind, "No longer do I call you servants, for a servant does not know what his master is doing; but I have called you friends, for all things that I heard from My Father I have made known to you."[113]

Jesus held back nothing His Father had given Him. He transparently made known His thoughts and broke the silence between God and man; between God and friends; even between God and enemies. No wonder His disciples were willing to give their lives for

Him. His naked vulnerability, not just on the cross of Calvary, but throughout their three and a half years with Him, affirmed His continual commitment to share His entire being with those He loved.

The sin of Judas was doubly hurtful when we realize Jesus had created an unparalleled atmosphere of openness and honesty amongst His disciples. He shared His heart, and each of His wounded followers had complete liberty to share as well. If someone sinned, all he had to do was admit his error and he would have been forgiven. No one suspected Judas would breach this trust and betray Jesus. It was unthinkable to imagine that this highly respected disciple would refuse this once-in-a-lifetime opportunity for full disclosure—this miraculous doorway into full acceptance and love. It was so unnecessary; so incomprehensibly shallow. All he had to say was, "I've been living a double life: stealing from our funds and harboring real bitterness toward you, Jesus. I am so sorry!" But, instead, he kept silent and allowed the cancer in his heart to contaminate his whole life, and destroy his destiny. Jesus disclosed this horrifying truth, "...how terrible it will be for my betrayer. Far better for him if he had never been born!"[114]

How many of us share our inner struggles and victories with others? Do we live such honest, open, and transparent lives for Jesus Christ that we are truly living epistles "known and read by all men?"[115] Are we, as born again Christians, willing to die to ourselves in order to break the silence of fear, doubt and unbelief; testifying of the marvelous victories God has accomplished in our lives and, even more importantly, our struggles? The cry of the psalmist echoes through the corridors of Heaven, "Let the redeemed of the Lord say so, whom He has redeemed from the hand of the enemy."[116] It's time to speak! It's time to break the silence!

ARE WE, AS BORN AGAIN CHRISTIANS, WILLING TO DIE TO OURSELVES IN ORDER TO BREAK THE SILENCE OF FEAR, DOUBT AND UNBELIEF?

OVERCOMING THE DEVIL

Why did Jesus come to this Earth? For one principle reason, with many marvelous over-
tones: "For this purpose the Son of God was manifested, that He might destroy the works
of the devil."[117] The devil, once named Lucifer, the morning star, is now known as Satan,
the archenemy of good. In eternity past, known as the anointed cherub and worship
leader of Heaven, he has been temporarily thrust down to the Earth awaiting his eventual
doom and eternal torment.[118]

The Bible clearly asserts there are only three possible ways to overcome the temptations
of Satan: "...they overcame [the devil] by the blood of the Lamb, and by the word of their
testimony and they loved not their lives unto the death."[119]

    a. **"the blood of the Lamb"**—There is only One spotless Lamb of God "slain from
       the foundation."[120] He took upon Himself the pain and punishment of our sin.

    b. **"the word of their testimony"**—The Greek word here is *marturia*, meaning evi-
       dence given, a record or report. It is referring to the record or report of what Jesus
       Christ has accomplished in rescuing our lives. The words *testimony* and *martyr*
       are derived from the same root word.

    c. **"loved not their lives unto the death"**—Only those who love the Author of life
       more than life itself can overcome the devil. Our broken and unashamed testi-
       mony, shared transparently with either friend or foe, is one of the clearest ways
       we can lay down our lives for Jesus Christ.

Only by embracing all that the shed blood of Jesus accomplished can each of us receive
a testimony worth dying for. But too many Christians, after being joyfully born into a
relationship with Jesus Christ, choose to remain silent, both about their struggles and
the astounding blessings we have been given as sons and daughters of God. The silence
must be broken, or the very rocks will scream out what God has done.[121]

NAKED, BUT NOT ASHAMED

All babies have two things in common; they are born clueless and clothes-less. The idea
that God is somehow squeamish about humans being naked is laughable. Whatever
we've got, God's seen it. But does this universal reality have an even greater significance
in the spirit realm? Let's go back to the first bodies. The Bible opens with the Book of Gen-

esis, in which the first human beings, Adam and Eve, were quite happy running around naked. Genesis 2:25 reads, "And they were both naked *[Hebrew—to be or to make bare]*, the man and his wife, and were not ashamed *[Hebrew—disappointed or confused]*."

God isn't a prude, Eve didn't blush, and Adam felt zero guilt when he looked at his naked wife. In a sinless, untainted world, nakedness was seen as the norm; viewed without a shred of shame, embarrassment or guilt. Was this atmosphere of, shall we say, full disclosure, limited to the physical dimension? Not at all! The original man and woman were completely open and honest with God and one another. Candor and honesty ruled, until deception and deceit attempted to overthrow the Kingdom of God.

Satan, appropriately titled the "father of lies,"[122] intentionally seduced our fore-parents, the first man and woman. Today, the seduction continues. Every day, fully imbedded within the surface morality of our culture, the devil offers godlikeness devoid of God. Situational ethics, intertwined in man-centered morality is the subplot behind much of today's music, movies and media. Our culture is a shell of what God intended.

So, is nakedness a good thing? Absolutely! In two particular situations: physically, between a husband and a wife; and metaphorically, in every healthy relationship available to man. As in the beginning, God wants us to be naked and transparent with Him; "And there is no creature hidden from His sight, but all things are naked and open to the eyes of Him to whom we must give account."[123]

Jesus affirmed this essential principle of transparency when He said, "No one, when he has lit a lamp, puts it in a secret place or under a basket, but on a lamp stand, that those who come in may see the light. The lamp of the body is the eye. Therefore, when your eye is good *[Greek—clear, properly folded together]*, your whole body also is full of light *[Greek—lustrous, bright, transparent or well-illuminated]*. But when your eye is bad *[Greek—hurtful]*, your body also is full of darkness *[Greek—opaque or impervious to light, so that images cannot be seen through it]*."[124]

Here's a paraphrase of these two verses, "When your vision is clear, then your life will be in order, fully transparent, bright and illuminated for others to see. But when your vision is blurred by hurt, then your life is opaque, impervious to light, so that others cannot see the person God intended you to be."

Perhaps, when Jesus said, "Satan has 'nothing in Me' "[125] He was implying, "There is nothing Satan can use against me because nothing is hidden." Jesus was saying. "What you see is what you get! My life is transparent, wide open for everyone, including My Heavenly Father to see!" It is God's will for all of us to one day join Him in saying and living the very same thing.

EVEL KNIEVEL TEACHES SUNDAY SCHOOL

I was ordained an Evangelist in November 1972. By 1977, my wife and I had become the pastors of Morning Star Ranch. By then the hippie trail had all but dried up, and our live-in community was mostly a refuge for people who were not stable enough to make it in a local church. So, from all over Northern California, churches sent hard cases our way; heroin addicts, alcoholics, prostitutes, pimps, those who had been in prison for ten to 20 years. Morning Star transitioned into what seemed at times like a maximum-security ministry, housing up to 75 people.

My wife, baby twin daughters and I lived on the property in the original run-down house that at one time had been a dorm for guys. I had slept there when I was first saved. How ironic! One day I'm a baby Christian sleeping in a bunk bed in a crowded house with 20 men. A few years later, I'm sleeping in the same house with my wife and children, except that now I have a new batch of people looking to me for help.

Suzie and I served as pastors of Morning Star for four years and four months; 52 months to the day—a complete season. But who's counting? I was. When the senior pastor of our home church had originally asked us to pastor there, he assured me it would only be for six to nine months. I was so unexcited about the prospect, I told him it was like asking Evel Knievel to teach Sunday School kids how to roller skate.

The last thing I wanted to do was squat among the sheep and scratch their wool. His response was a bullet from God, "Francis, the Bible does not say, 'the Lord is my evangelist, my prophet, my teacher.' It says, 'the Lord is my Shepherd,' and if you don't get a shepherd's heart, you're not going very far in God." Ouch! I knew God needed to do a heart transplant in my narrow little life; it was everything I never wanted and more.

The transparent life was knocking at my door. Opening it would cost me dearly, but be well worth the investment. If we refuse to share our lives in a vulnerable way with sick souls, they will be unable to see Jesus in us. "Follow me as I follow Christ"[126] requires incredible openness.

The Psalmist writes of God, "He sent His word, and healed them, and delivered them from their destructions."[127] As God spoke the world into existence, so we too, have the privilege of obeying the Holy Spirit and seeing light shine in our darkness. Living an honest and transparent life should be our goal, and words are often the method God uses to demonstrate this.

SEARCHING FOR REALITY

In 1981 the Ranch was closed down, and my wife and I headed into many years of itinerant evangelistic ministry. Frankly, I was chomping at the bit to tour the world and take a shot at transforming the greater church world. I was pregnant with a vision to see the Body of Christ authenti-cally representing the One who had rescued my life. It was a consuming passion; having seen a measure of fruit on a local level, my overwhelming burden was to see the Church equipped to be like Jesus. No small task.

However, almost two decades later, having ministered to hundreds of thousands of people in hundreds of churches and in many nations, I left the road with a somewhat jaded but optimistic desire to start a stream of churches. My hope was that these churches would model the most Christ-like qualities my wife and I had observed in the healthiest people and churches over the years.

As Jesus was beginning His earthly ministry, He went into the synagogue on the Sabbath day, and then stood up to read, "The Spirit of the Lord is upon Me, because He has anointed Me to preach the gospel to the poor; He has sent Me to heal the brokenhearted, to proclaim liberty to the

IF WE REFUSE TO SHARE OUR LIVES IN A VULNERABLE WAY WITH SICK SOULS, THEY WILL BE UNABLE TO SEE JESUS IN US.

captives and recovery of sight to the blind, to set at liberty those who are oppressed; to proclaim the acceptable year of the Lord."[128]

Jesus came to bring good news to a world intoxicated with evil; to heal, liberate, and deliver. He offered a hand of complete forgiveness and acceptance to everyone in His fallen creation. It took unparalleled courage to say what had never been said; to live like no one had ever lived, and to die a death like none before—all for love; all for us.

STARVING FOR LOVE

A young boy grew up with a father who beat him mercilessly every day, demanding absolute obedience. While still in his youth the boy wanted to become a priest, but over time the terrible relationship with his overbearing and unaccepting father gradually caused his heart to harden.

On the last occasion his father beat him, he resolved not to cry—and he didn't. His father never hit him again. But hundreds of millions of people around the world have wept over the subsequent actions of this one love-starved boy—Adolph Hitler.[129] How would history have been rewritten if only Hitler had been healed from his father's wounds. In the end, hurt people, hurt people; and healed people, heal people.

Though everyone in our culture is talking about love, few are experiencing the real deal. More often than not, what is called love is the counterfeit, sugarcoated, eye-candy variety whose satisfaction rate can be measured in seconds. Yet real love still beckons, offering each of us an immeasurable return on our heart-felt investment.

George Gallup, Jr., the world-renowned pollster, lists six basic inner needs found throughout society. They are:

1. To believe that life is meaningful and has a purpose.

2. For a sense of community and deeper relationships.

3. To be listened to and to be heard.

4. To feel that one is growing in faith.

5. To be appreciated and respected.

6. For practical help in developing a mature faith.

Genuine Christians living transparent and caring lives have the grace and God-given capacity to live the life described in the Gallup survey. We as Christians have found the meaning and purpose of life. By God's matchless grace, we have been drawn into a community of ever-deepening relationships, where everyone cannot just be listened to, but heard. We have been called to be a loving fellowship where each person can feel they are growing in faith; and where all are appreciated and respected as they mature in faith and love by knowing and living for Jesus.

In 2005, as I was greeting Hurricane Katrina evacuees who were standing in a food line in Mississippi, an elderly African-American lady looked into my eyes and said, "You're one of the those walk-the-talk Christians aren't you?" Her words were like arrows to my soul; I looked back into her perceptive eyes and said, "I'm trying to be." I could barely keep from crying. Isn't that what our hearts long for, being walk-the-talk Christians? If the world could see in us the love and care their hearts are longing for, they would then want to meet the God we claim to know.

IDENTIFICATION THROUGH TRANSPARENCY

Kenneth Burke was perhaps the foremost teacher of rhetoric, the art of using language effectively and persuasively, in the 20th century. He believed the key term for the old rhetoric was *persuasion,* and the key term for the new rhetoric is *identification.* Burke regarded *persuasion* as the communicator's attempt to get the audience to accept his or her view of reality as true, whereas *identification* is the common ground that exists between

IT TOOK

UNPARALLELED

COURAGE FOR JESUS

TO SAY WHAT HAD

NEVER BEEN SAID;

TO LIVE LIKE NO ONE

HAD EVER LIVED, AND

TO DIE A DEATH LIKE

NONE BEFORE—ALL

FOR LOVE; ALL FOR US.

speaker and audience. If the audience can see their lives in you, you will see the spark of life in them.

Burke believed the link between speaker and listener was called *substance*. He used the word substance as an umbrella term to describe a person's physical characteristics, talents, occupation, background, personality, beliefs and values. The more overlap there is between the substance of the speaker and the substance of the listener, the greater the *identification*.

Each week at The Rock of Roseville, we invite a person whose life has been transformed by Jesus Christ to come and share their journey with us. We call it "My Story." Each individual is asked to write a 600-word testimony focusing on approximately 40 percent past problems, 50 percent present victories, and ten percent what life at The Rock of Roseville has done for them. As it is the high point of each service, it is positioned right before the message.

The profound impact of identification can be seen in the Book of Ruth. Ruth pledges solidarity with her mother-in-law, Naomi: "For wherever you go, I will go; and wherever you lodge, I will lodge; your people shall be my people, and your God, my God."[130] That was identification; and without identification there is no persuasion.

Do people identify with our churches, or has the rhetoric been so persuasion centered, that we somehow think people will receive the essence of our message even when the essence of our lives is unrelatable to them? Jesus was the most authentic, genuine person who ever walked the face of the earth, and if we have any hope of representing Him effectively on this earth, our lives must in some way model that same level of humble integrity as well. Christ in you, your only hope of glorifying God.[131]

I love the way Tim Keel sums up this point: "It's easy to be a preacher; all you have to do is stand in front of your people and open your vein. But that requires discernment and vulnerability."

FROM SICK-OF-LOVE TO LOVESICK

When I first gave my heart to Jesus, I was so burned out on my attempts to find true love, that I remained celibate for three years until my marriage to Suzie—no dating, no flirting, just Jesus. The selfless love He freely offered was so refreshing to my weary soul, it immediately replaced the self-centered love to which I had been accustomed. I was learning about a whole new kind of love; where "in lowliness of mind... each esteem*[s]* others *[as]* better than himself."[132] I was soon to realize that everything God does is designed to lead us into intimacy with Him.

Old Testament marriages were often business arrangements that parents made for their children. So the soon-to-be husband and wife didn't like each other? No problem. They would learn to work things out.

But Solomon and his Shulammite bride were a different story. They wrote the book on romance. The account in Song of Solomon of the impassioned love between a husband and wife matches the relationship Jesus longs for with His Church. In desperation the bride says, "I looked for him but did not find him. I will get up now and go about the city, through its streets and squares; I will search for the one my heart loves... When I found the one my heart loves... I held him and would not let him go."[133]

Why are we not "lovesick"[134] when we stray away from our Lord? It's not because He doesn't love us enough. The groom says, "Sixty queens there may be, and eighty concubines, and virgins beyond number; but my dove, my perfect one, is unique."[135] Amazing but true, that is each one of us, seen from God's perspective.

We can never know God's love until we fail and then realize He is still madly in love with us. As Mike Bickle so often says, "God is not just a God of love, He is a God in love." He has never held back in sharing His impassioned love for us. Likewise, we should not refrain from continuously giving our heartfelt love to Him. At times our love will be expressed in an honest heart of worship; at other times it will be demonstrated in a vulnerable testimony of God's saving grace.

A DEATH DEFYING LEAP

In 1967, Charles Murray was training as a high diver for the '68 Summer Olympics. During that season of his life, a Christian friend regularly talked with him about his need for a personal relationship with Jesus Christ. Though Charles insisted he was not ready to give his life to Jesus, one day he called his friend and wanted to know where to look in the New Testament for some verses about salvation.

Late that same night, Charles decided to go to the pool and practice his diving. His Olympic status gave him special privileges to use the University pool even during off hours. The pool area had a ceiling of glass panels, and on this particular night a full moon illuminated the pool sufficiently for him to dive by moonlight.

Enjoying the atmosphere, Charles climbed to the highest platform in the darkness to make his first dive. As he did, the Spirit of God began to convict him of his sin. All of the Scriptures he had read that day began to flood his mind. Going to the edge of the platform, he turned around and faced the wall, preparing to dive backwards.

Spreading his arms to gather his balance, Charles gazed at the wall. He was stunned by what he saw; the light of the moon caused the silhouette of his outstretched arms to form the shape of a cross. Instantly, Charles was overcome by his sin. His heart was so broken by the convicting power of the Spirit he immediately sat down on the platform and prayerfully asked Jesus to forgive him and save him.

Suddenly, the lights came on. An attendant had come in to check the pool area. As Charles looked over at him, he happened to look down into the pool. To his shock and horror, he realized the pool had been emptied of all its water. It had been drained that day for repairs. God had saved his life that day in more ways than one. Charles had nearly jumped to his death, but the cross had spared him. His miraculous rescue affirms what Paul wrote in his letter to the Corinthians, "For the message of the cross is foolishness to those who are perishing, but to us who are being saved it is the power of God."[136]

May we each one day kneel in humility before our faithful Creator and surrender to His will for our lives. Only then will we have the potential to live the fully transparent, bright and illuminated lives God intended for us. "This is the message which we have heard from Him and declare to you, that God is light and in Him is no darkness at all. If we say that we have fellowship with Him, and walk in darkness, we lie and do not practice the truth. But if we walk in the light as He is in the light, we have fellowship with one another, and the blood of Jesus Christ His Son cleanses us from all sin."[137] Giving in to darkness will eventually kill us. In contrast, only by surrendering to Jesus Christ, the true Light of the world, can we be saved.[138]

If we can learn to live in the light, we won't ever have to fear the darkness.

SUMMARY POINTS

- Living an honest and transparent life should be our goal, and words are often the method God uses to demonstrate this.

- If the world could see in us the love and care their hearts are longing for, they would then want to meet the God we claim to know.

QUESTIONS FOR DISCUSSION

1. What do you consider to be your greatest weakness? Why do you think that? How do you think God could use this weakness to help others?

2. What aspect of living a transparent life is most frightening? Most appealing? How is God challenging you to be more transparent?

3. Think of a person who has modeled transparency for you. How has their transparency impacted your life? How did your feelings for them change after they shared transparently with you? How did others respond to their transparency?

4. What are the areas in your life you are most concerned will hinder you from fulfilling God's will? How do you think they will hinder God's will? How is God helping you to change them?

5. Are there any areas in your life that you are still too ashamed to share with others? How is God bringing healing to you in those areas?

CONFIDENT OF
GOD'S INTENTION

CHAPTER SEVEN

WHEN PERSPECTIVE TRIUMPHS OVER CIRCUMSTANCE

"All truth passes through three stages.
First, it is ridiculed. Second, it is violently opposed.
Third, it is accepted as being self-evident."

Arthur Schopenhauer

CLARITY IS OVERRATED

A man visited the House of the Dying in Calcutta, India, for three months, to find out how to best spend the rest of his life. When he met Mother Teresa she asked, "What can I do for you?" He asked her to pray for him.

"What do you want me to pray for?" she responded. He then shared the most pressing burden on his heart, "Pray that I may have clarity."

Mother Teresa responded firmly, "No, I will not do that." Surprised, he asked her why. She told him, "Clarity is the last thing you are clinging to and must let go of."

"But," he told her, "you always seem to have the clarity I long for." She laughed and said, "I have never had clarity; what I have always had is trust. So I will pray that you trust God."

Trust is believing that God has all the clarity we need for every situation in our lives.

At times He shares this clarity with us, and on other occasions He withholds it for a more suitable time. Proverbs alludes to this mystery when it says, "It is the glory of God to conceal a matter, but the glory of kings is to search out a matter."[139] The times for concealing and revealing are always in the trustworthy hands of God.

The reason we do not trust God is because we do not know Him. Just as you can only trust someone you know, the reverse is also true; you cannot know someone unless you first trust them. If we knew God we would certainly love and trust Him; and that means trusting Him to reveal understanding to us in His timing, not ours. The trusting person is the one who is no more attached to God giving him clarity than God staying silent.

THE REASON WE DO NOT TRUST GOD IS BECAUSE WE DO NOT KNOW HIM.

Most people traveling on commercial airplanes never ask the pilot what he is doing. Instead, we trust that the person in the cockpit is fully competent to handle any and all emergencies. If the weather rattles us a bit, we still believe the plane will remain intact, and the pilot will guide us safely home. The track record of the airline only adds to our confidence; an impeccable safety record further enhances trust. It is the same way with God. Speaking through the psalmist, the Spirit of God issues an eternal promise; "Once I was young, and now I am old. Yet I have never seen the godly forsaken...."[140] The more we know God the more we trust Him.

More than anyone else in our lives, God wants to continually commune with us. Moses and Joshua understood this. "So the Lord spoke to Moses face to face, as a man speaks to his friend. And he would return to the camp, but his servant Joshua the son of Nun, a young man, did not depart from the tabernacle."[141] Real trust is no longer being dependent upon God's blessing, but upon being desperate to know God Himself. Blessings can be misinterpreted, whereas our trust in someone we know remains unshakeable.

1 Peter 1:7 in the King James Version of the Bible refers to "...the trial of your faith, being much more precious than of gold...." The Greek word for trial in this verse is *dokimion*, which by implication means trustworthiness. The trials of life reveal our trust in God, and therefore are the most valuable lesson we can learn in life. Until we esteem the promises in God's Word above our own thoughts, we will continue to chafe whenever something goes contrary to our expectations.

God provides a reality check of who He is in the Book of Isaiah, "For My thoughts are not your thoughts, nor are your ways My ways," says the Lord. "For as the heavens are higher than the earth, so are My ways higher than your ways...."[142] I don't need to figure out what's going on as long as I trust the God who already knows.

Because Mother Teresa loved the life God gave her, she was able to love the people God sent her. Less than five feet tall and slightly more than 100 pounds, this giant of a woman fully accepted everyone and everything God sent her way. Mother Teresa held on tightly to who God made her to be and embraced the outrageous circumstances she encountered, turning impossible situations into divine appointments. She saw God in her circumstances, because she was willing to see her life from God's point of view. We will only be able to see God working in our lives when we can see our lives from God's perspective.

In a video about her life, Mother Teresa looked confidently into the camera and said, "...be where He wants you to be. If He puts you in the street; if everything is taken from you and suddenly you find yourself in the street, to accept to be in the street at that moment. Not for you to put yourself in the street, but to accept to be put there. To accept if God wants you to be in a palace, well then to accept to be in the palace as long as you are not choosing to be in the palace.

"This is what makes the difference in total surrender; to accept whatever He gives, and to give whatever it takes with a big smile. This is the surrender to God. To accept to be cut to pieces and yet every piece to belong only to Him. This is the surrender. To accept all the people that come, the work that you happen to do. Today, maybe you have a good meal and tomorrow maybe you have nothing. To accept and to give whatever it takes. If it takes your good name, if it takes your good health. That's the surrender. That is it. You are free then." Time and again Mother Teresa's Christ-like perspective triumphed over her circumstances.

MOMENTARY LIGHT AFFLICTIONS

THE CHALLENGE COMES, NOT IN THAT WE HAVE PRESSURES, BUT IN HOW WE VIEW THEM.

Earth is short; Heaven is long, and what happens here doesn't stay here. We will either take it with us as an eternal reward or an everlasting regret. Our time here is actually the shortest chapter of our endless lives, but it is also the one that will set the tone for eternity. While it is appropriate to rejoice in its brevity, it is wise to be concerned with its finality.

Let the Apostle Paul's words lift your spirits, "Therefore we do not lose heart. Even though our outward man is perishing, yet the inward man is being renewed day by day. For our light affliction *[Greek—pressure, anguish, burdens, trouble],* which is but for a moment, is working for us a far more exceeding and eternal weight of glory…"[143] The eternal glory that will be revealed in our lives will so far outweigh the challenges of this momentary world; the end result will be worth every pressure and burden we have gone through.

The challenge comes, not in that we have pressures, but in how we view them. If they are anchors around our necks weighing us down in despair, then we are missing their point entirely. Instead of sinking us, the pressures in our lives actually anchor us to the One who loves us most. With this perspective, pressures become weights we not only need, but also should wholeheartedly welcome.

Just as beauty is in the eyes of the beholder, bondage is as well. I have a choice in how I see my life. Most of the time,

I choose to see my life from God's point of view. "Now thanks be to God who always leads us in triumph in Christ, and through us diffuses the fragrance of His knowledge in every place."[144] I was made to triumph with Him—always and forever.

On the other hand, we are what we think. If we think we are afraid, then so we are. Proverbs says it so clearly. "For as he thinks in his heart, so is he."[145] I need to think God's thoughts, not my own. I need the mind of Christ, not the mind of Francis. I must learn to "cast [my] burden on the Lord and let Him sustain [me]."[146] As Kenneth Hagin Sr. has said, "I am concerned, but it's not my concern."

One of history's men of faith experienced firsthand the saving grace of God in extraordinarily challenging situations. "...king [David]...said, 'As the Lord lives, [He] has redeemed my life from every distress....' "[147] Likewise, in the Book of Samuel, he again reiterates this same unshakeable conviction, "...David answered...them, ' "As the Lord lives, [He] has redeemed my life from all adversity...."'"[148]

The difficulties David faced were daunting and overwhelming, traversing his entire life. Here is but a sampling: David accepted and defeated the challenge of the giant Goliath;[149] he pretended to be insane in front of King Achish;[150] he hid in the caves of Adullam from King Saul,[151] and when his son Absalom wanted to overthrow him and have him killed,[152] David placed his trust in the living God.

Over and over again, David was delivered from one impossible situation after another. He knew how temporary and light every affliction really was. No trial would alter his unshakeable conviction.

Once, when I was preaching on this subject, halfway through my message, I took off my outer shirt to reveal a T-shirt that, in giant letters, read, "I have no problems!" I know it shocked and perhaps irritated some people in the meeting who thought I was crazy. Was I living in denial or deception? I then told the audience, "I'm living a stress-free life; a pressure-free existence, snuggled in the hollow of God's hand. What I have is not only possible; it's essential for each of you. I invite you to join me."

I then turned away from the audience and displayed the backside of my shirt that read, "God's got a lot of problems and I'm praying for Him." The audience laughed at this tongue-in-cheek expression, but they understood my point. If I am truly "casting all of my cares upon the One who cares most for me,"[153] then why am I not living the carefree life? If I am indeed challenged by Scripture to be "anxious for nothing,"[154] then my goal is not to let even one drop of anxiety touch my heart and mind.

IF ONLY...

Have you ever looked back on a situation in your life in which you wish you could get a "Do Over"? I have, many times.

Growing up, my twin brother and I had a very competitive relationship. What one of us could do, the other was determined to do better! Once, in my early teens, my brother dared me to go down a steep hill on my bike without using any brakes and make a 90-degree turn into our driveway. After watching him successfully maneuver the seemingly impossible feat (I found out later he was braking with his hidden right hand), it was my turn.

There I went, screaming down the hill. By the time I reached the driveway, I quickly realized I had absolutely no chance of making the turn, and so I did the only thing I could do—I froze. My bicycle then hit a one-foot-high wall separating our neighbor's driveway from our own at approximately 300 mph. Together, my bike and I did a complete somersault in the air, sailing over the adjacent driveway and finally landed in a large pile of jagged rocks.

Lying bloodied and bruised, I glanced over to see my brother Joseph sprawled out on our front yard, roaring with laughter. He said it was the funniest thing he had ever seen: me upside-down on my bike with a look of sheer terror etched on my face. Our motto back then was, "It's not funny until someone gets hurt, and then it's hilarious." When my brother realized how serious my injuries were, he did become more sensitive, accompanying my mother and me to the hospital. Fifteen stitches, and several decades later, I now laugh about the prank, but back then I wanted an immediate do-over. That, of course, was impossible.

Like myself, many people suffer from an acute case of the "if onlys." If only I were smarter; had more money; were prettier; had a different body; could lose weight; could get married; wasn't married; had a baby; didn't have children; had a different job; had a job;

hadn't made that mistake; had a best friend; could go back in time; married a different person; or were raised differently. If only God would do this one thing for me. If only, if only, if only....

Our lives are not a waste of time; everything we go through has value! God perfects us through our difficulties. "So even though Jesus was God's Son, He learned obedience from the things He suffered."[155]

Difficulties don't produce character; they reveal it.

DIFFICULTIES DON'T PRODUCE CHARACTER; THEY REVEAL IT.

There is purpose in every setback. In Matthew 26:31–32, Jesus was aware that His sudden arrest and crucifixion would wreak havoc on His disciples. Therefore He told them, "All of you will be made to stumble because of Me this night, for it is written: 'I will strike the Shepherd, and the sheep of the flock will be scattered.' But after I have been raised, I will go before you to Galilee." Learn to look past your setbacks and you will discover the purpose in your pain. If you are focusing on your pain, you are still living in the past. No good can come from watering last year's crop. The ancient philosopher Euripides once wrote, "Waste not fresh tears over old griefs."

INDISPENSABLE PAIN

Ashlyn Blocker is fearless, say her parents and kindergarten teachers. Her fearlessness is not courage based; it is because she cannot feel pain. When she eats at the school cafeteria, teachers have to put ice in her chili so she doesn't burn her mouth. Five-year-old Ashlyn would never know until the damage was done and she had swallowed the chili scalding hot.

Over the few short years of her life, Ashlyn has chewed through her tongue while eating, and torn the flesh off her finger, not realizing how she was hurting herself. Only a few people have ever been diagnosed with what Ashlyn has—anhidrosis, or CIPA—a rare genetic disorder giving her a congenital insensitivity to pain.

Looking at photos of Ashlyn over the years you can trace the history of self-inflicted injuries. One of the pictures shows her in a Christmas dress, hair beautifully fixed, with a swollen lip, missing tooth, and puffy eye. With her hands wrapped in athletic tape to protect them, she smiles gleefully like a boxer who just won a prizefight.

Ashlyn's mother, Tara Blocker, provides further understanding for all of us as to why pain is so essential for life, "Pain's there for a reason. It lets your body know something's wrong and it needs to be fixed. I'd give anything for her to feel pain."

Why do we resist the gift of pain? Why do we second guess the perfect plans of an omniscient Creator? Our shallow understanding merely consigns us to miss the point of purposeful circumstances, needlessly repeating the learning process tailor-made for each of our precious lives.

The inability to feel pain is not new. For thousands of years lepers have reaped the tragic fruit of life without the sensation of pain. Leprosy is a chronic infectious disease which attacks the skin. Cuts and bruises are not felt, and often get infected because the person is unaware he is hurt. Each year more than two million people worldwide are diagnosed with this sensory loss, which left untreated will cause parts of the body to become deformed or even die. Throughout history lepers have been rejected outcasts, isolated in colonies where they often died with little or no treatment and care.

Many times in life we naively pray, "Lord, if I just didn't have to experience so much pain, my life would be great." In truth, it is the pain of life that keeps us humble, increases our dependence upon God and others, and causes us to reconsider foolish actions that can damage and destroy our lives. Pain protects us.

Malcolm Muggeridge, the famous British journalist and author, wrote near the end of his life, "Contrary to what might be expected, I look back on experiences that at the time seemed especially desolating and painful with particular satisfaction. Indeed, I can say with complete truthfulness that everything I have learned in my 75 years in this world, everything that has truly enhanced and enlightened my experience, has been through affliction and not through happiness."[156]

SURF'S UP

Oswald Chambers in his classic devotional, *My Utmost For His Highest,* wrote, "Huge waves that would frighten an ordinary swimmer produce a tremendous thrill for the surfer who has ridden them. Let's apply that to our own circumstances. The things we try to avoid and fight against—tribulation, suffering, and persecution—are the very things that produce abundant joy in us. 'In all these things we are more than conquerors through Him who loved us.'[157] In all these things, not in spite of them, but in the midst of them. A saint doesn't know the joy of the Lord in spite of tribulation, but because of it. Paul said, 'I am exceedingly joyful in all our tribulation.' "[158] Enjoying life means we are living "in joy" and not "in confusion or frustration."[159]

In eternity, those who know the Lord will be eternally grateful for each trial encountered on earth. All tests and trials are flawlessly conceived and executed by a benevolent Creator. Every struggle in life is tailor made with us in mind, perfectly crafted by the Master surgeon Himself, with no possibility of malpractice—no chance of difficulties not working for our good.

Challenge your inner man, moment by moment, to return to the One who loves you the most. Train your soul in the way that it should go and when you are older your soul will not depart from the path of life. This is crucial because you are the most out-of-control person you have ever known. So am I. I am constantly training my soul; doing all that I can to keep my eye focused on God alone, so that my whole body is filled with the light of His presence.

The psalmist captured the essence of soul therapy. "Return to your rest, O my soul, for the Lord has dealt bountifully with you."[160] The Lord does not deal more bountifully with one person over another. Certain people are just more successful in seeing their perspective triumph over their circumstances.

PLANNED HAPPINESS

A man in his early 90s lost his wife of 60 years. Realizing he could no longer care for himself, he decided it was time to move into a nursing home. On the morning of his first day, he arrived at eight o'clock sharp, neatly dressed and clean-shaven, with his hair meticulously in place. Legally blind, he sat for many hours in the lobby patiently waiting for his appointment.

When he was finally told where his room was, he smiled sweetly and began to maneuver his walker toward the elevator. While en route, the attendant escorting the elderly gentleman provided a verbal description of his tiny room. After hearing a brief assessment of the room's contents, the new tenant enthusiastically replied, "I love it."

Surprised at his response, the employee said, "Mr. Brown, you haven't even seen the room; just wait."

Without missing a beat, the man replied, "That doesn't have anything to do with it. Happiness is something you decide on ahead of time. Whether I like my room or not doesn't depend on how the furniture is arranged...it's how I arrange my mind. I already decided to love it. It's a decision I make every morning when I wake up. I have a choice; I can spend the day in bed recounting the difficulty I have with the parts of my body that no longer work, or get out of bed and be thankful for the ones that do. Each day is a gift, and as long as my eyes open I'll focus on the new day and all the happy memories I've stored away, just for this time in my life."

What a tremendous outlook! Too many people spend their lives questioning if God really is concerned about their happiness. It all depends upon how we view happiness. If we define it as "a self-centered quest for personal fulfillment," then, it is true, that would not be God's objective for our lives. But, if we define happiness as the *World English Dictionary* does, then happiness is more than just a mere possibility, it is God's will for our lives.

The *World English Dictionary's* defines happy as:

1. feeling or showing pleasure, contentment, or joy;

2. causing or characterized by pleasure, contentment, or joy;

3. feeling satisfied that something is right or has been done right;

4. resulting in something pleasant or welcome.

The elderly man in the story had it right—happiness is
not having what you want; it's wanting what you have.
Thus, happiness is available to everyone—it's just a new
perspective away. Nothing about the above definition
requires selfish ambition or addiction to circumstances
in order to fulfill happiness.

As Paul challenged us to be "exceedingly joyful in all
...tribulation,"[161] so too we can rise above life's natural
malaise and experience the supernatural presence of God
in every situation. His grace is more than sufficient, if we
allow His strength to rise above our weakness.[162]

In the end, how we respond to life is far more important
then what happens to us. Oswald Sanders described it in a
slightly different way, "Maturity is moving from a thin skin
and a hard heart to a thick skin and a soft heart." A good
attitude has no expiration date; like fine wine, it gets better with age. In our brokenness, let us lift our eyes to God,
for from Him alone comes our help.[163]

That part of each of us that wishes things would get better
is not our friend. Actually, that is our enemy. I have no idea
what "better" looks like; I can barely brush my teeth.

God has no intentions of fulfilling my expectations, but
every intention of fulfilling His expectations through me.

I don't know what's best for me—never have, never will. I
don't even know enough to have a strong personal preference. Spending my life wishing things would work out is
an enormous waste of my time. The smartest thing I can
do when it comes to how I would like things to work out
is to remain neutral: no bias, fully flexible, and yielding
to the will of the Father. God's been God for a long time;
He's really good at it.

THAT PART OF EACH OF US THAT WISHES THINGS WOULD GET BETTER IS NOT OUR FRIEND. ACTUALLY, THAT IS OUR ENEMY.

I need the same amount of faith to welcome the life God gives me, as I needed when I first embraced the God who saved me. We know we are trusting God when we stop wishing our lives would change. Love the life you have and joyfully receive every meal placed before you. My wife's pragmatic father would say to all four of his children seated around the dinner table when they would begin to complain about what was put before them, "Eat it! Your mother doesn't make anything that's not good." In life, God has never prepared anything for us that will not work for our good, no matter how it tastes.

STORM CHASERS

Mountain Mike, a dear friend of our family, earned his nickname because he is one of the most knowledgeable men alive about the Sierra Nevada mountain range. A former member of the U.S. Ski Team, Mike Shreve has lived his whole life in South Lake Tahoe and seen more snowstorms than he can remember. Located at 6,500 feet above sea level, Lake Tahoe has numerous ski resorts that provide some of the best skiing on Earth.

GOD HAS NO DESIRE TO GIVE YOU PEACE FROM THE STORMS OF LIFE. HIS PLAN IS TO GIVE YOU PEACE IN THE STORM.

One Christmas, as we were visiting, he told me, "Heavy winters bring more bountiful summers." The comment sparked a revelation. We all appreciate spring flowers and summer fruit, but it's the dying in the fall and the storms of winter that bring the most bountiful harvests. Our failure to fully appreciate the storms of life merely demonstrates how shortsighted we really are. Interestingly, the opposite is also true; an over-dependence upon temporary satisfaction invariably leads to future disappointment. Bless the storms in your life, and stop chasing fleeting pleasures.

Mike also shared with me, "Every storm feels the same coming in; whether it brings two inches of snow or two feet." We never know which storm will bring the most challenge or the most benefit to our lives. Therefore, embrace storms as they come; there are no accidental storms.

Likewise, God has no desire to give you peace from the storms of life. His plan is to give you peace in the storm. Peace that comes when the storm stops is temporary. Learning to have peace during the storms of life is far better. We were created to meet Jesus in the middle of our storms. Frankly, few of us have time for Him outside of the storms of life.

My wife once told me about a women's conference she attended where one of the messages was entitled, "Stop Barking at Your Bowl." The speaker used an illustration about her dog during the session. When it was time for her dog to eat he would run over to the bowl and begin to bark at it, thinking the bowl was the one who fed him. God showed her that at times we do the very same thing. We bark at our circumstances, trying to make them change, rather than look to God who alone provides for all our needs.

DRIVE INTO THE WIND

A pastor friend of mine used to live in the Yukon Territory, in northern Canada. One winter day he went hunting on snowmobiles with a couple of natives.

Hours into their journey a violent storm came upon them. After a long period of fighting the snow, their lead guide gestured for the three of them to stop and talk. With howling winds and piercing snow buffeting them, they huddled together. The guide confessed, "I think we're lost. I've grown up here my whole life, and I've never seen this rise in the terrain before." At those words the pastor's heart sank. Their guide was renowned. For him to be lost in a blinding snowstorm was terrifying and unexpected. After a few moments of reflection, the pastor sheepishly said, "We need to pray." Bowing their heads in desperation, they asked the Lord for His mercy and guidance.

Following an emotional prayer, one of them spoke up, "I believe we've been going in the wrong direction. Because of the intensity of the storm, we've been going with the wind. What we need to do now is drive directly into the wind and snow." For a few moments after this unorthodox declaration they remained silent. Everywhere they looked was unfamiliar. In the middle of the whiteout, all they could hear was the sound of the howling wind and their pounding hearts. Each came to the jarring realization that either this radical recommendation was a Word of Knowledge, or it would lead them to certain death, going farther and farther away from safety until they would run out of gas.

After another desperate prayer, they decided to receive the counsel and headed off full-throttle into the utter unknown. Though the wind and snow continued to batter them, they steadfastly drove directly into the storm. An hour or so passed when, finally, the guide stopped, knelt down and brushed away the snow from beneath them. He could see from the color beneath their feet that they were on a frozen body of water. He then told his companions, "Since we are on water, I believe I know where we are." He proceeded to lead them safely home.

What had saved their lives? In addition to the marvelous grace of God, they had been willing to do what hurt the most: face their fears and drive directly into the unknown. We only change when our willingness to accept God-allowed pain exceeds our fears. At times in our lives, we will all suffer a sharp painful disillusionment before we fully surrender. Even Jesus had to endure a painful crucifixion before He could say, "It is finished!" As we keep our eyes on the prize, we will eventually see all of the pressure and pain pale in comparison to the glory that will be revealed in us.[164]

My prayer is that the Lord will help each of us to see Him working in every moment of our lives. That He will lead us to trust that, the plan we cannot see is greater than the circumstances we can.

SUMMARY POINTS

- Trust is believing that God has all the clarity we need for every situation in our lives.

- The more you know God, the more you will trust Him.

- Difficulties don't produce character; they reveal it.

- God has no intentions of fulfilling my expectations, but every intention of fulfilling His expectations through me.

- Heavy winters bring more bountiful summers.

QUESTIONS FOR DISCUSSION

1. What areas of life do you easily trust God with? What areas are more difficult for you to put your trust in Him? In what ways is God challenging you to trust Him more?

2. When thinking of your most significant regret, how have you come to terms with it? How has God used this life experience to impact other's lives?

3. What is your perspective of your current circumstances? In what ways do you think God wants you to change your perspective? What are some strategies that would help you see things more like God does?

4. Describe the current challenges in your life. How are you responding to them? Well? Poorly? How do you see God using these challenges to change you to be more like Him?

5. Describe a setback in your life that you now see God used to bring purpose and blessings.

CHAPTER EIGHT

FINDING PLEASURE
IN YOUR PAIN

UNTHINKABLE JOY

Dr. Bob Pierce, founder of World Vision, a Christian relief organization, tells of an extraordinary event he witnessed with his own eyes. During the Korean War in the early 1950s, tens of thousands of refugees fleeing from the Red Chinese army attacking the north poured into South Korea. Under siege, in the middle of a freezing winter, the embattled city had lost all electric power. While other facilities in Seoul remained closed due to the upheaval, the churches opened their doors, having all night prayer meetings entreating God for His mercy, protection and grace.

At four o'clock one morning, a dark, unbearably cold church was filled with multitudes of refugees. Women who had watched their homes burn and their husbands tortured to death sat in the frigid building holding their children close. Most were dressed in nothing but thin, padded cotton. The worship that night was filled with tears streaming down many faces. In the midst of this traumatic scene, the pastor of the church decided to take an offering for the hundreds of refugees still coming into the city.

With great passion he entreated, "Something must be done to help those who are coming to us. What does this congregation have to give?" Those shivering in the crowded pews had lost their homes, businesses, and savings, and were themselves in desperate need.

The pastor continued, "...and so we will give an offering of clothes." It seemed an unthinkable request; insensitive to the obvious needs of the people surrounding him.

Yet the pastor's appeal brought an extraordinary response. For a few anxious moments no one moved. Finally, an elderly, emaciated man came forward, removed his vest, and solemnly laid it on the communion table. A young mother took the sweater off her baby and tucked the infant inside her own clothes. The tiny sweater joined the tattered vest. Soon, the table was piled high with clothes.

Their lives were shattered and broken, but these nameless saints counted it all joy to literally give the clothes off their backs. If joy is how God responds to life, and if He is truly living in us, then joy must be how we respond to life as well.

Paul the Apostle endorsed this seemingly irrational line of thinking when he wrote, "I am exceedingly joyful in all our tribulation *[Greek—pressure, affliction, anguish, burdens, persecution, trouble].*"[165] Is it possible to be grieved and joyful simultaneously? Absolutely! You might be brokenhearted someone has died, yet joyful he or she is in Heaven. You might be saddened your job is ending, but joyfully confident God has something better.

Faith is the miraculous ingredient that activates true joy in each of our lives. Whereas *happiness* sometimes waits to see what is going to happen, *joy* blissfully opens its arms to every moment, choosing in advance to see life from God's point of view.

The Bible gives us the perfect response to the calamities of life: "Weeping may endure for a night, but joy comes in the morning."[166] Yet it is possible for us to resist the joy that God desires to bring to us. Joy only comes in the morning, if we choose to let joy come in the morning. We can opt to let fear or worry come in the morning, or perhaps even depression and suicide. If we so desire, we can invite *discouragement* for breakfast, take *hopelessness* out to lunch, and join *despair* for a candlelight dinner. It's our call. I have spent enough time with each of these pathetic emotions. Now I limit my life experiences to seeing joy in my circumstances.[167] It is my choice how I choose to see the life God has given me.

Joy has to be invited into our lives and, once invited, must not be taken for granted. Just as Jesus focused on, "...the joy that was set before Him *[and]* endured the cross...,"[168] we must concentrate on the joy set before each of us as we endure the hardships in life.

Jesus took pleasure in His pain, and embraced the purpose behind His suffering. May God open our eyes to see that glorious purpose in our life as well.

When we spend our lives dwelling on yesterday, we shouldn't be surprised if tomorrow never comes. Instead of embracing what is happening in our lives, many of us feel empty about what is not happening. There's a better option: the next time you are going through hell, don't stop. We have a fanciful expectation of what we think we need, and when it doesn't take place we are disappointed. As God gives each of us the life He knows we need, we must therefore learn to embrace life as it is, not as we wish it were.

THE CURE FOR THE SHATTERED LIFE

In 2 Corinthians 12:10, Paul the Apostle writes, "Therefore I take pleasure in *[Greek—think well of, approve, am pleased with]* infirmities, in reproaches *[Greek—insults, hurts]* in needs, in persecutions, in distresses *[Greek—calamities, anguish]* for Christ's sake. For when I am weak, then I am strong."

Did he really mean pleasure? Was Paul exaggerating when he said he thought well of, approved of, and was pleased with his insults and hurts? Or had his perspective been so radically transformed he actually found pleasure in being persecuted and insulted? It seems evident from scripture that Paul found the God of comfort in an extraordinary way in the midst of the distresses and calamities assaulting his soul.

So, what's the cure for a shattered life? Once again, it's the three-letter word: joy. Based upon my knowledge of Scripture and my experience living the Christian life, I would personally define joy as a deep sense of inner ela-

WHEN WE SPEND OUR LIVES DWELLING ON YESTERDAY, WE SHOULDN'T BE SURPRISED IF TOMORROW NEVER COMES.

tion and satisfaction that comes from seeing your life from God's perspective, and responding properly to the challenges and suffering of life.

James, the brother of Jesus, taught the importance of responding well to suffering when he wrote, "My brethren, count it all joy *[Greek—cheerfulness, calm delight, gladness]* when you fall into various trials *[Greek—adversities, temptations]* knowing that the testing of your faith produces patience *[Greek—cheerful or hopeful endurance]*. But let patience have its perfect work, that you may be perfect and complete, lacking nothing."[169] Who wouldn't want to be "perfect, complete, and lack nothing?" Yet, things coming up roses will not make this happen; we must allow situations to, at times, come up thorns.

Catherine A. Miller, a missionary to Africa, wrote a poem entitled "Other Than Mine" that deeply impacted my life. She wrote:

> I would have chosen a sunlit path all strewn with roses fair.
> With never a cloud to darken my way, nor a shade of anxious care.
> But He chose for me a better way, not sunshine or roses sweet.
> But clouds o'er head and thorns below that cut and hurt my feet.
> I have such joy of another kind: my Rose of Sharon is He.
> And as for sunshine, His lovely face is perfect sunshine to me.
>
> I would have chosen my life to be active, tireless and strong.
> A constant, ceaseless, working for Him amid the needy throng.
> But He chose for me a better lot, a life of frequent pain
> Of strength withheld when needed most and loss instead of gain.
> He gave me work of another kind, far, far above my thoughts.
> The task of interceding with Him for souls that He had bought.
>
> Tis far, far better to let Him choose the way that we should take.
> If only we'd leave our lives with Him, He'd guide without mistake.
> We, in our blindness would never choose, a pathway dark and rough.
> And so we would never find in Him the God who is enough.
> In disappointment, trouble and pain, we turn to the changeless One,
> And find out how faithful, loving and wise is God's beloved Son.

Recently, after receiving some jolting news that could have been seen as sad and disappointing, the Holy Spirit quickly reminded me of my only responsibility. I was in charge of the Respond Well Department; He was in charge of everything else. The world says, "Be in control." The Word says "Give God control."[170] What a relief! What a joy!

FINAL FRUIT

In 1921, a couple named David and Svea Flood went as missionaries from Sweden to the Belgian Congo, in the heart of Africa. Along with two other missionaries, the couple was sent to minister in a remote village. The chief of the village would not let them enter because he was afraid of angering the local gods.

So the two couples built mud huts just down the road and prayed for a spiritual breakthrough. But none came. For years, the only contact the missionaries were allowed to have with the villagers was with one young boy who delivered them food. So Svea Flood, a tiny woman, only four feet, eight inches tall, decided that if this was the only African she could talk to, she would try to lead the boy to Jesus. That she did, but, much to the chagrin of each missionary, there were no other salvations.

In time, malaria struck the four missionaries. The second couple, being well enough to travel, decided they had had enough suffering. They packed up their marginal belongings and retreated to the mission station. David and Svea Flood, however, remained to minister alone.

Soon after the departure of their friends, Svea found out she was pregnant. When the time came for her to give birth in the middle of this remote wilderness, the village chief softened enough to allow a midwife to help them. Tragically, after their little girl was born, Svea was so exhausted and weak from battling malaria that she only lived 17 more days.

Svea's husband, David, was devastated. He dug a crude grave, buried his 27-year-old wife, and went back down the mountain to the mission station. He then gave his newborn daughter to the other missionary couple, and said, "I'm going back to Sweden. I've lost my wife, and I can't take care of this baby. God has ruined my life." He left Africa, rejecting not only his calling, but God Himself.

A few years later, the new parents of the baby died of a mysterious disease. The baby girl, Aggie, now three years old, was then given to an American missionary couple who eventually brought her back to the United States. Living in America, they raised Aggie in a godly Christian home.

Twenty-five years passed.

One day a Swedish Christian magazine mysteriously appeared in Aggie's mailbox. She had no idea who had sent it, and of course she could not read the words. But as she turned the pages, she saw a photo of a grave with a white cross, and on the cross the words "Svea Flood"—the name of her mother.

Aggie rushed to find someone who could translate the article. It told the story of two missionaries who had come to a village in the Belgian Congo a very long time ago. A baby was born, the mother had died, and one little African boy had been led to Christ. After all the whites had left the area, the boy grew up and went on to lead the chief and 600 people in the village to Jesus. The article ended, "all because of the sacrifice of David and Svea Flood."

A few years later, while Aggie and her husband were attending an evangelism conference, Aggie heard a report about the Belgian Congo. The head of the national church, representing some 110,000 baptized believers, told how the gospel had spread throughout his nation. After the message, Aggie approached the leader and asked him if he had ever heard of her parents, David and Svea Flood.

The man was stunned. "It was Svea Flood who led me to Jesus. I was just a boy in our village when she befriended me." Overcome with emotion, the national leader embraced Aggie in a long, sobbing hug. Then he implored her, "You must come to Africa to see for yourself. Your mother is the most famous person in our history."

When Aggie and her husband traveled to the nation, they were welcomed by thousands of cheering villagers.

Later, Aggie visited her father in Sweden. The God who heals had mended his broken heart, allowing him to be reunited in love and forgiveness with his long-lost daughter.[171]

The Psalmist writes, "You will show me the path of life; in Your presence is fullness of joy...."[172] In the fullness of time, somewhere down the marvelous path of life, there is a place of understanding, a place of joy. Only in the fullness of time will all that we have gone through make sense. Every tear, every sorrow, every painful mystery in our lives will fill a divine tapestry, and reveal the perfect plan of God for each of our lives. Don't write off your struggles too quickly; there is hidden treasure, soon to be revealed and forever cherished.

TRIAL BY FIRE

I once traveled across three time zones to speak at a church. Arriving late on a Saturday night, I was picked up the next morning by the senior pastor's 80-year-old father. Having had very little sleep, I was barely aware of my surroundings when we pulled on to a narrow two-lane levee. There was an old pickup truck in front of us moving rather slowly, so my elderly escort moved into the other lane to pass the truck. However, after clearly passing the vehicle, he did not return to our lane.

It seemed strange that he remained in the oncoming lane, but it became outright disconcerting when I saw a large truck coming toward our car. The truck was getting closer, and there was still time to go back into the right hand lane, yet he did not budge. Suddenly, I felt as if everything was moving in slow motion. Doesn't he see the truck? What is he thinking? Do I tell him to turn back into our lane? I had just met him, but should I yell at him to turn?

Paralyzed in indecision, I waited until the last possible moment for him to make a move. Now, our situation was beyond desperate. In one sweeping motion, I grabbed the wheel and jerked our car back into our lane. The oncoming truck went speeding by us, blowing his horn and wondering if we were out of our minds. I knew I wasn't, but serious doubts had just been raised about the man driving me.

After a few awkward moments, I began to half-apologize to the elderly gentleman for seizing the wheel. Had I overreacted? Was he just about to turn in? I sat, now fully awake, and wondered. My question would be answered a few minutes later.

After leaving the levee, we were about to turn onto a freeway when I realized he was entering a ramp with large signs screaming, "WRONG WAY! DO NOT ENTER." At that moment, all the lights were on; I knew he was going to kill both of us if I didn't do something. I yelled, "Please stop the car! Please pull over! I'm sorry, but we are going onto a freeway in the wrong direction. I really do need to drive." It was unimaginably awkward, even mortifying, but it needed to be done. I did everything I could to get this precious man to go in the right direction, but he just could not.

On that unforgettable day, going in the wrong direction almost cost me my life. It wasn't the first time. I had spent years dodging the bullets of my poor choices. Even as a Christian, I mistakenly stayed far too long in the lanes of self-deception.

In the early years of my Christian life, I spent many days praying for my difficulties to end, hoping the gracious God of Heaven would end the overwhelming struggles in my life. When, in time, my prayers for relief seemed to be answered, almost immediately I would find something else to ask God to deliver me from. It was an addictive cycle of missing the point of my struggles.

The Apostle Peter understood as well as anyone the purpose of his pain when he wrote, "Beloved, do not think it strange concerning the fiery trial which is to try you, as though some strange thing happened to you; but rejoice to the extent that you partake of Christ's sufferings, that when His glory is revealed, you may also be glad with exceeding joy."[173] We are free to rejoice; free to be glad with exceeding joy. We are honored to partake of Christ's suffering. It is not strange; it is glorious. Suffering for Jesus provides incomparable satisfaction. All we need are eyes to see, ears to hear, and a tender, faith-filled heart to embrace.

Mike Bickle provided further insight when he wrote, "Satisfied people sin less. Much of the sin in the body of Christ is a wrong response to pain, fear and the need for comfort. Sin is a false comfort that people use as a prop to get them through seasons of pain. Many people get into sin because they feel beaten up and abandoned by God and men. Even though they are not truly abandoned, they feel that way. So they reach out for immediate comfort in status, financial gain or wrong expressions of sexuality."[174]

There is a much better alternative. "Therefore let those who suffer according to the will of God commit their souls to Him in doing good, as to a faithful Creator."[175] A revelation of God's heart will lead to an appropriate commitment of our own lives, and the absolutely faithful response of a

> "SATISFIED PEOPLE SIN LESS.... SIN IS A FALSE COMFORT THAT PEOPLE USE AS A PROP TO GET THEM THROUGH SEASONS OF PAIN."
>
> —MIKE BICKLE

loving Creator. We know we are walking in resurrection life when we are more concerned about Heaven than Earth and more interested in trusting God than understanding life's most asked question, "Why is this happening to me?"

The Apostle Paul concludes, "If then you were raised with Christ, seek those things which are above, where Christ is, sitting at the right hand of God. Set your mind *[Greek—affections]* on things above, not on things on the Earth. For you died, and your life is hidden with Christ in God."[176] Dead men have no preferences. They bask in total acceptance and complete resignation; as R.I.P. implies, they rest in peace. It is God's will for each of us to have no preferences, not just when our bodies die, but when we choose to die to our own will and yield to Him.

DROWNING

What keeps us from finding the hidden treasures in our pain? Why do our hearts flinch when tested? Is it because we fear the unknown, or because we fail to trust the God we should know? Are we drowning in worry and unbelief, unable to see the infinite wisdom and eternal value of the suffering that God has tailor-made for each of us? We must learn to die gracefully. Yet this goes against our natural instinct to survive. But what good is survival if it means living less than God intended?

Sebastian Junger, in his best-selling book *The Perfect Storm*, that was later made into a successful movie, describes the sequence a person goes through while drowning. Interviews with individuals who had drowned, but were resuscitated, chronicle every dimension of their chilling experience.

When a person begins to drown, the first emotion they experience is *disbelief*. They can't believe this is really happening to them. It is quickly followed by a sense of *desperation*. Next, there is a feeling of *awkwardness*; no one drowns gracefully.

Drowning invariably comes at an *inopportune* moment. A person drowning may think, "I can't die; I have tickets to the big game next week." This is followed by an acute sense of *embarrassment*. In their imagination, they see people shaking their heads because their death was so senseless. They feel stupid, and may think, "This is my last, great act of stupidity." Finally, as shocking as it may sound, after about 90 seconds, while still conscious, the drowning person takes in an *involuntary breath of water*.

Though it is unnerving for us to imagine ourselves drowning in water, it is equally disconcerting to watch someone drown in the perilous waters of life. The water-related sequence described above has many similarities to the stages an emotionally despondent person goes through when they despair of life.

IN OUR MANGLED WORLD, THERE IS NO SHORTAGE OF PEOPLE WHO FEEL AS IF THEY ARE DROWNING... EVERY DAY, PEOPLE DROWN IN HOPELESSNESS AND DESPAIR.

In our mangled world, there is no shortage of people who feel as if they are drowning due to addictions, or because of poor moral, relational, or even financial choices. Every day, people drown in hopelessness and despair. Embarrassed by how messed up their lives have become, they often feel stupid for blowing it so badly. Always awkward, emotional drowning never comes at a convenient time. It is the last experience people want to have. Yet, God yearns to teach us a better response. One that defies hopelessness, laughs at calamity, and leads to a fearless life of peace and tranquility.

POLAR TWINS

A father had twin boys who were polar opposites. One was an optimist, believing everything would turn out great. The other was a pessimist, convinced that things always ended poorly.

One day, the father decided to do an experiment and placed each of the young boys in separate rooms. He put the pessimist in a room packed with every imaginable fun toy. On the other hand, he left the optimist in a room with just a giant bag of horse manure.

An hour later, the dad returned to the pessimist's room only to find the boy had not even touched the toys and was sitting idly in a corner. Dumbfounded, the father asked his son why he wasn't playing. Shrugging his shoulders, the boy replied, "Well, if I start playing with them I'll probably get bored or hurt myself, so I figured why even start?" Stunned at the pessimistic son's response, the father left the room shaking his head in disbelief.

Entering the other son's room, the father was shocked to find the optimistic twin completely immersed in the giant bag of manure. He was literally swimming in it; thrashing around as if searching for a ten-carat diamond. The father asked, "What are you doing?" His son looked up and grinned, "There's just gotta be a pony in here somewhere!"

Long ago, I settled in my heart to live as an optimist. I want to live life enthusiastically, wading through disappointments and delights alike. I am constantly seeking God's best for my life and for those I am called to serve.

Paul the Apostle, also an optimist, once wrote, "Now thanks be to God who always leads us in triumph in Christ, and through us diffuses the fragrance of His knowledge in every place."[177] *Always* and *every* are serious words. If Paul meant *sometimes* or *periodically* instead of *always* he would have said that. If instead of *every place* he meant *some places*, he would have written that. But Paul wrote the truth; he stood on what God alone can promise and deliver, "There's got to be a pony in here somewhere." Finding that pony may take a lifetime and may look quite different than we think, but an overcoming, optimistic attitude will make all the difference.

LOSING ALL—BUT NOT EVERYTHING
Paul and Betty Neff were a happily married couple. Shortly after Betty had her first baby, she had a dream in which she went to Heaven. There, she saw Jesus standing on a hill with four children on His right side and another adult on His left.

Years later, in 1983, Betty and her husband Paul lost four of their five children when their home burned down just days before Christmas. In the blazing inferno, after rescuing one of his children and attempting to save the other four, Paul suffered serious burns and injuries. He almost severed one of his arms, and broke his back in so many places falling out a window, that doctors said he would never walk again. Against his doctor's orders, Paul insisted on going to his four children's funeral a few days later. Still battered by his many injuries, Paul had to be wheeled in on a gurney in order to attend the memorial.

Seven years later, Paul and Betty's only remaining child was killed in a tractor accident. Now, all five of their children had died. The trauma of these losses would be enough to send the strongest of couples plummeting over an emotional abyss. Yet, Paul and Betty knew the God in whom they believed, and were persuaded that He was able to keep what they had committed to Him.[178]

Without any living children of their own, Paul and Betty chose to receive a powerful ministry from God. They regularly began to scan newspapers across America for individuals who had lost multiple members of their families in tragic accidents. They then would contact them, offering whatever assistance they could.

How can someone overcome such potentially life shattering setbacks and yet transition into what they consider their life's calling? It doesn't just take the grace of God; it takes our willingness and commitment to receive that grace. Paul the Apostle was able to overcome excruciating reversals in his life because he chose to receive God's grace instead of resisting it. He wrote, "We then, as workers together with Him also plead with you not to receive the grace of God in vain."[179]

I once read of a couple who had their only child of three years drown in a pond near their home. Overcome with grief, they felt unable to go on with life. After writing a suicide note, the crushed parents committed suicide together. How tragic! There is a loved One in Heaven who longs to give us all we could ever need, not just enabling us to survive our tragedies, but to thrive in them. God promises us, "As we know Jesus better, His divine power gives us everything we need for living a fruitful, godly life...."[180]

No God = No Peace.
Know God = Know Peace.

OVERCOME GRIEF WITH JOY

The emotions of life are many and complex. One moment we are being overcome, and the next we are overcoming. As the Psalmist once wrote in the depths of despair, "Have mercy on me, Lord, for I am in distress. My sight is blurred because of my tears. My body and soul are withering away. I am dying from grief; my years are shortened by sadness. Misery has drained my strength; I am wasting away from within."[181]

How ironic that, just two verses prior, he had written, "I am overcome with joy because of your unfailing love, for you have seen my troubles, and you care about the anguish of my soul."[182] It seems the choice of being overcome by joy or despair is ever before us. If there were nothing to overcome, as in the Garden of Eden prior to the Fall, then we would have no reason to fight for joy. Like ripened fruit, it would just fall from the trees of life.

But such is not the case.

Choosing fruit from the Tree of Life or the Tree of the Knowledge of Good and Evil each day remains in our court. Though what happens in life may seem to be completely out of our control, how we view life is always our choice. I can choose to see my life from God's expansive, life-giving point of view, or be limited by the myopic narrowness of fear, unbelief and ignorance which can only lead to emotions of panic, despair and anger. For many of us, this is how we face our challenges. We are unable or unwilling to defeat the emotional onslaught seeking to destroy our lives; or we can look up, past the distracting struggles that keep us stuck in the past, bound in the present, and lacking hope for our future. May we resign ourselves in advance that whatever comes our way, we are choosing to remain "…steadfast, immovable, always abounding in the work of the Lord, knowing that your labor is not in vain in the Lord."[183]

GIVE IT AWAY
Years ago, precious friends of ours had a daughter, Shari, and son-in-law, Philip, who were living for a season as missionaries in Africa. While stationed there, Shari gave birth to a child. With limited medical facilities available, when the newborn suffered complications they were unable to get the necessary care to save the child's life. Had the baby been born while Philip and Shari were back in the U.S., they would have had far better medical facilities to save their baby's life. But this was not meant to be.

THOUGH WHAT HAPPENS IN LIFE MAY SEEM TO BE COMPLETELY OUT OF OUR CONTROL, HOW WE VIEW LIFE IS ALWAYS OUR CHOICE.

Such a devastating experience could have sent the young couple into great despair, becoming bitter toward God. It could have, as is the case with many parents who lose a child, destroyed their marriage. But Philip and Shari chose to see their pain from God's point of view. At the height of their personal grief, God spoke to their hearts these profound and comforting words, "When you lose something, you don't know where it is. But when you give it away, you always know exactly where it is." Holding on to this truth, their hearts were free to respond to this tragedy as God intended. But their incomprehensible pain was not over.

A short time later, the oldest of their children was diagnosed with a rare brain disease, and after a long illness he, too, died. Once again, when their hearts were overwhelmed, God led them to the rock that was higher than their pain.[184] Though their hearts had been broken, Philip and Shari accepted God's unusual plan for their lives and chose to go forward instead of wallowing in their grief. As the Apostle Peter once wrote, "Therefore let those who suffer according to the will of God commit their souls to Him in doing good, as to a faithful Creator."[185]

Each of us will come to a sudden fork in the road of life. One branch will lead to pain without purpose; the other will lead to pain with a plan. That true road can only be walked by faith, and will eventually lead to indescribable peace.

Pain is up ahead for all of us. We cannot avoid it. But we can choose to view pain from God's eternal perspective and reap the benefits of a life fully yielded to a God worth trusting.

The promise of Scripture strengthens our hearts, "...God is faithful, who will not allow you to be tempted beyond what you are able, but with the temptation will also make the way of escape, that you may be able to bear it."[186]

SUMMARY POINTS

- *Joy* is the cure for the shattered life. Joy could be defined as "a deep sense of inner elation and satisfaction that comes from seeing your life from God's perspective, and responding properly to the challenges and suffering of life."

- Every tear, every sorrow, every painful mystery in our lives will fill a divine tapestry, and reveal the perfect plan of God for each of our lives. Don't write off your struggles too quickly; there is hidden treasure, soon to be revealed and forever cherished.

- If I am really "crucified with Christ," then I have no preferences. Dead men don't have preferences.

- We can choose to view pain from God's eternal perspective and reap the benefits of a life fully yielded to a God worth trusting.

QUESTIONS FOR DISCUSSION

1. When you reflect upon a very painful life experience, do you think God was responsible in some way? You were responsible? Others were responsible? Describe the experience and how if has affected your life.

2. What is your typical reaction to pain? In what ways do you try to avoid pain? When you are in pain, how do you cope?

3. When you read 2 Corinthians 12:10, "Therefore I take pleasure in infirmities, in reproaches, in needs, in persecutions, in distresses, for Christ's sake, for when I am weak, then I am strong," what is your reaction? In what ways can you live this scriptural principle in your own life?

4. What is your view of weakness? How do you feel about your own weakness? What is your view of weakness in others? How do you think God feels about your weakness?

5. As you think about the pain in your life, can you also see the "hidden treasures" within the pain? Please explain. What strategies could you implement in your life that could help you see these "hidden treasures" more readily?

CHAPTER NINE

I LOVE MY LIFE !

WHOLE LIFE IN A HALF BODY

My wife and I once had lunch with a 24-year-old Christian lady in New Zealand named Debbie Ward. Aside from a strikingly joyful countenance, what made Debbie unique was the fact that that she was born with no lower half of her body: no feet, no legs, nothing below her waist. At the time we met Debbie she had been traveling around her nation speaking to groups of young people. She told us she began each talk by saying, "Don't feel sorry for me! I love my life!"

She was so confident and wise in her convictions you couldn't help but realize she indeed had been blessed with something special from God. Half a body had not limited her from having twice the character of most people. She loved her life; not just any life, but the one God gave her. In the same way Jesus gave Stephen a standing ovation in Heaven,[187] I believe this precious young lady will receive one too. Every time she confesses, "I love my life," she becomes the tallest person in the room.

Trials are meant to bring out the best in us, not the worst. Oswald Chambers writes, "God does not give us overcoming life: He gives us life as we overcome."[188] You were created to overcome. The discouragements of yesterday don't disqualify you, the setbacks of today can't sabotage you, and the failures of tomorrow won't finish you. Every challenge in life is designed to reveal our weakness and God's strength and to make us realize not just how desperately we need Him, but how absolutely sufficient His grace is in each of our lives.

OUR STRENGTHS ARE FAR MORE DANGEROUS THAN OUR WEAKNESSES, PROVIDING THE EASIEST ACCESS TO FAILURE. IT IS OUR WEAKNESS THAT HOLDS THE KEY TO UNLOCK THE GRACE OF GOD.

Most people miss one of the great paradoxes of life, erroneously believing the doorway to their successes will be through their strengths. Not so! Our strengths are far more dangerous than our weaknesses, providing the easiest access to failure. It is our weakness that holds the key to unlock the grace of God. The Apostle Peter once wrote, "God resists the proud, but gives grace to the humble."[189] If pride is intrinsically resistible, then humility must, by its very nature, be *irresistible.* Humility is learning to fully embrace and delight in our weakness. It is that captivating quality of Jesus that releases the irresistible grace of God.

People's desires are not God's desires. They'll do anything to change the way they look—to change the shell—when God wants to transform the pearl. Cosmetic surgery will never make someone whole. Wholeness must be internal. In this age of genetic engineering, stem cell research, and designer children, we continue to substitute the Creator's flawless intent for our flawed perceptions.

Dream God's vision for your life, not a temporary one. It is pointless to complain about your job; instead, begin crying out to God for a new heart. We don't need a new life; we need to appreciate the one God has given us. The problem is, most people don't appreciate what they have. More often than not, we would gladly give up our own lives for the life of another. But in doing so we fail to realize we would be exchanging the life we have been given, that has been especially designed for us, for the life specifically designed for another. This is one of the key ways God uses celebrities: they show the world you can have everything in the physical world and still be unfulfilled. Embrace the life God has given you, not the life you think you should have.

Like Lucifer of old, who attempted to re-create the Universe in his own likeness saying, "I will ascend... I will be like the Most High...."[190] we have lost almost complete sight of what we have been given. Our inner longing to become Designer-Creators has evolved, in essence, out of godless self-promotion; attempting to birth children fashioned in our own image, even in the likeness of the shallow qualities that impress us but bore Heaven.

I remember reading about an elderly American woman who died of starvation alone in her apartment because she didn't have any money. Yet when the police examined her belongings, they found over $100,000 in cash buried inside the mattress she died on. The woman had stashed it away and then forgot about it. Our heavenly Father has buried amazing gifts deep inside each of us, yet how many of us have tragically lost sight of them?

Do we know what the God who shows no partiality[191] has equally dispensed to each of us? Do we love the life He has given us, or are we obsessed with what we don't have? The perfect promise in 2 Peter 1:3 should be a pledge written on our hearts: "...His divine power has given to us all things that pertain to life and godliness...." God has given us everything we need to love the life He has given us. Batteries are included!

CORRECTING GOD'S MISTAKES

A few years ago a person started attending our church. She immediately began to selflessly serve. We all loved her. She went to membership class and then asked for a meeting with my wife and me. When Suzie and I met with her, she disclosed that she had been born a man. She had been married to a woman for seven years, but had a sex-change operation. He—I will now use his proper gender—wanted us to accept him as a woman.

For the next few months we met with him regularly for counseling. We kept his situation confidential from everyone except for a handful of senior leaders. We gave him a key to a private restroom, and asked him to no longer attend women's meetings. Suzie and I had many tearful discussions about God's heart for him. We offered financial support to send him to a Christian ministry that specialized in helping individuals who struggled with their sexual identity; he refused to go. We also found many testimonies of individuals who had struggled in the same area and allowed God to heal their troubled hearts. He read them, but was not persuaded.

As we searched the scriptures,[192] we realized that by altering his body, he had made himself a eunuch—"a man or boy whose testicles have been removed or do not function."[193]

He was no longer completely a man, nor would he ever be a woman. We shared scriptures encouraging him to be a eunuch in the house of God,[194] and promised to stand by him as he walked through whatever was ahead. Over and over again we expressed our love and commitment to remain proudly by his side throughout the entire process. But in the end, his deception prevailed. He would often say to us, "I was born with a birth defect, and so I corrected it." We assured him that God doesn't make mistakes. It wasn't his body that needed to be changed but his heart that needed healing.

How we respond to events in our lives is far more important than what actually happens. No aspect of our lives has ever been an oversight to God. "My frame was not hidden from You, when I was made in secret...."[195] God has never made one mistake concerning our fragile lives. "...I am fearfully and wonderfully made... and that my soul knows very well."[196] There has never been a recall of even one human being; all of us have been given infinite potential by a gracious God.

If we refuse to accept God's plan for our lives, we consign ourselves to a brave new world of perpetual unfulfillment. Waiting for a better life is like staring at your dinner, hoping to improve its taste. God's will is that we would come to the place where we love the life He has given us, instead of wishing for what does not exist and would not satisfy us even if it did. There is no faster way to get to where your heart really wants to be than through the will of God. Accepting and embracing the will of God is the Express Train to Fulfillment.

In life there are no shortcuts, only detours. Even if we momentarily transition into being pleased by life's circumstances, it will be short-lived. May we each accept the obvious: God is trying to change us, not change the world around us. In life, if we cannot appreciate what we have, we will never be pleased with what is ahead. If we cannot grow where we are, we will never bear fruit elsewhere.

Even those born with catastrophic physical deformities can be a catalyst for compassion, generosity and joy. Traumatic difficulties are not a roadblock to personal fulfillment. Seen from God's perspective, they can even become the doorway to a transformed life.

The primary reason people do not love the life God has given them is because they do not know and trust God. When we don't trust God, inevitably, we begin to play God ourselves. Judas thought he knew better than God the Son, as did King Saul, King Solomon and most of the kings of Israel and Judah. So many people have died unfulfilled, having spent a lifetime envying others, when God Himself is the only Person worthy of our worship.

Our misunderstanding of life should never tempt us into thinking God has lost His underlying sense of purpose for us. "Trust in the Lord with all your heart; do not depend on your own understanding."[197] The more I know me, the less I trust me; the more I know God, the more I trust Him.

"It is better to trust in the Lord than to put confidence in man."[198]

"Blessed is that man who makes the Lord his trust...."[199]

That's when the joy comes. Only by completely trusting God can we become joyful. "But let all those rejoice who put their trust in You; let them ever shout for joy, because You defend them; let those also who love Your name be joyful in You."[200]

Jesus went one step further when He challenged each of us to the core. "Simply put, if you're not willing to take what is dearest to you, whether plans or people, and kiss it goodbye, you can't be My disciple."[201]

WE ARE ALL FRUIT INSPECTORS

I know I am a fully surrendered Christian when my desires have changed into God's desires. If we claim to be a Christian and have not had a dramatic change of heart, we must accept the obvious: we need to be born again. Jesus said,

THE PRIMARY REASON PEOPLE DO NOT LOVE THE LIFE GOD HAS GIVEN THEM IS BECAUSE THEY DO NOT KNOW AND TRUST GOD.

"...a tree is known by its fruit."[202] If we have been born again in the past, but our lives demonstrate little fruit, the ball is still in our court. Apparently, we must be born again—again.

According to Christian pollster George Barna, more and more people are confessing they are born again but fewer are living differently.

MORE AND MORE PEOPLE ARE CONFESSING THEY ARE BORN AGAIN BUT FEWER ARE LIVING DIFFERENTLY.

Born again Christians are defined by Barna as people who said they have made a personal commitment to Jesus Christ and it is still important in their life today. They also indicated they believe that when they die they will go to Heaven, because they had confessed their sins and had accepted Jesus Christ as their Savior. Respondents were not asked to describe themselves as born again.

In his report on the state of Christianity in America, Barna writes, "The worst thing would be for millions of people to accept Christ as their Savior, and then live the remainder of their life as if nothing had changed other than their eternal destiny. The challenge to faith communities, at this point, is to help people realize that you cannot be a follower of Christ by taking the free gift of salvation and then continuing to pursue the same life trajectory as before making that decision. Embracing Christ as your Savior is not the end of the story. It's the very beginning point of a transformed life that centers on constant worship of God, serving other people, investing personal resources in the values of God, deepening their relationship with God every day, and creating families that place God at the center of their shared experience."

Jesus provoked each of us when He proclaimed, "Most assuredly, I say to you, unless one is born again, he cannot see the kingdom of God. Nicodemus *[a Pharisee]* said to Him, 'How can a man be born when he is old? Can he enter a second time into his mother's womb and be born?' Jesus answered, 'Most assuredly, I say to you, unless one is born of water and the Spirit, he cannot enter the kingdom of God. That which is born of the flesh is flesh, and that which is born of the Spirit is spirit. Do not marvel that I said to you, 'You must be born again.' "[203]

When we receive God's Spirit, only then do we begin to see with God's eyes, and to feel with His heart. Until Jesus is Lord of our lives, all we will ever be able to become is religious—going through the motions of performing for God, but not knowing Him. We miss what life is all about. We miss having a deep, personal relationship with our Creator. "...the Lord spoke to Moses face to face, as a man speaks to his friend."[204]

Jesus Christ's warning 2,000 years ago remains as potent as ever, "Not everyone who says to Me, 'Lord, Lord,' shall enter the kingdom of Heaven, but he who does the will of My Father in Heaven. Many will say to Me in that day, 'Lord, Lord, have we not prophesied in Your name, cast out demons in Your name, and done many wonders in Your name?' And then I will declare to them, 'I never knew you; depart from Me, you who practice lawlessness!'"[205]

Knowing God is not an option, it is a necessity. If we are truly born again, our desire to draw close to God will grow in allowing Him to take His rightful place as the Lord of our lives. God has done everything He can to invite us into intimacy with Him. "Draw me away! We will run after you. The king has brought me into his chambers. We will be glad and rejoice in you...."[206] True relationship leads to intimacy with God, which in turn always leads to becoming more like His perfect Son, Jesus.

I'D BE A LOUSY GOD

I would be a terrible God. I know this is true based on how I treat my friends when they are in trouble. I tend to want to bail them out of every crisis they encounter. Thus, being God, I would spoil the whole planet. Not only do I not know what is best for me, I rarely know what is best for others.

In the movie *Bruce Almighty*, the title character is frustrated by how God is running his life. Bruce's adamant complaint leads to a sovereign test. God allows him to become God for a season, and grants Bruce the ability to decide how to answer the prayers of an entire planet. Completely overwhelmed by the multiplied millions of requests pouring in, Bruce finally says, "Yes!" to everyone's prayers, no matter how selfish or shortsighted they may be. Only then does he realize that what he thought would help actually hurts—badly. Chaos ensues as every self-centered motive in the hearts of men is revealed. In the end, Bruce humbly repents for his misjudgment, and returns the reins to God.

The more I live, the more I realize there is no crisis I can fix. I will always need God. Though it is a natural human desire to meet someone else's need, the complexity of doing that is beyond my comprehension. God is infinitely more interested in fixing us than in fixing our problems. As a matter of fact, He is often the author of our problems. We're saying, "God, stop the problem!" He's saying, "Stop the whining and begin to understand what I am allowing."

When Jesus faced the greatest trials of His life, He didn't try and manipulate His Father in Heaven to lighten His load. Instead, Christ's pain only further revealed His true purpose in life. "Now My soul is troubled, and what shall I say? 'Father, save Me from this hour?' But for this purpose I came to this hour."[207] We were born for trouble; created for a fight. It is only through trouble that our soul is formed, shaped, and molded into the image of an untroubled God. I love the overstated expressions: "Don't give me any good news, it only weakens me," and, "If you are not living on the edge, you are taking up too much room."

Remove your troubles and you eliminate your purpose in life: to be conformed to the image of Jesus Christ, "For whom He foreknew, He also predestined to be conformed to the image of His Son...."[208] Defining your purpose in life reduces frustration. Being created in the image and likeness of God[209] was the beginning of your purpose. Finishing that work is now your destiny; it is where God is taking us. Your purpose is part of the reason why God is taking you there. Anything that keeps you from fulfilling God's ultimate purpose—being conformed to His image—must be disregarded and treated as a distraction. Tragically, most people live and die distracted.

As I look back over my life, my consistent appeals for God to make my life easier have not fallen on deaf ears due to indifference. The all-knowing, all-caring God has merely dismissed my fleeting requests as narrow-minded, showing a lack of foresight and long-term planning. He has refused to bow to my ignorance, but has instead held fast to His wisdom. He knows the easy life would destroy my potential; therefore, He makes my life purposefully difficult.

Only by pressing the olive is the oil poured out; only by crushing the flower is the true fragrance released. Only as Paul was "...pressed out of measure...insomuch that we despaired even of life..."[210] did the "...sweet-smelling aroma, an acceptable sacrifice, well pleasing to God"[211] come forth from his life.

TO LIVE IS CHRIST—TO LAUGH IS GAIN

If you pieced together the common perceptions of Jesus, He would come out looking a lot like a mortician—morbidly serious. Mouth bent permanently down in a mournful frown; more at home in dark, dead places than out in the sunshine. The typical religious picture of Jesus suggests a man born without a funny bone in His body.

Some would consider it sacrilegious, even blasphemous, to believe that Jesus often told jokes and used humor when ministering to others. But consider this: how often do children stampede a funeral home just to spend time with the mortician? Young people are incredibly perceptive. They know how to spot life, warmth, genuine affection—and that's why they flocked to Jesus. They didn't come to receive some mandatory religious instruction; they came because they enjoyed His company and felt His love.

Without a doubt, because Jesus loved life, people loved Jesus!

Paul's letter to the Philippians actually states that "to die is gain."[212] Yet, while the title of this section twists the Scripture, it is not an unbiblical concept. Haven't we each heard of people who died laughing?

Jesus died on the cross "for the joy set before Him."[213] Paul the Apostle, destined to suffer much for the sake of Christ, confessed, "I die every day."[214] The Apostle Peter, who died being crucified upside down, was motivated throughout his afflictions by this biblical hope: "So be truly glad! There is wonderful joy ahead, even though it is necessary for you to endure many trials for a while."[215]

It has often been said that the shortest verse in the Bible is "Jesus wept."[216] However, upon closer examination you will find that "Rejoice evermore"[217] is even shorter. It has two words in the Greek, as compared to three in the former. Both emotions have their place. But there is no doubt about which emotion we will experience forever. "And God will wipe away every tear from their eyes; there shall be no more death, nor sorrow, nor crying. There shall be no more pain, for the former things have passed away."[218]

I am not suggesting that Jesus was a comedian, relying on one-liners to pave the way for the Kingdom. His crucifixion and the events leading up to it were more tragic than we will ever understand. Isaiah prophetically identified Him as "a man of sorrows."[219] Yet Christ's suffering and grief, while paramount in importance, were balanced by a clear sense of humor. Jesus loved the life He had been given; that was His great attraction.

The following are all examples taken from Jesus' teachings. Imagine how these illustrations would have struck his audience:

- If we hide our light under our bed, Jesus reminded His listeners, we might burn our house down.[220]

- Jesus chided the Pharisees for filtering tiny gnats out of their drinks while swallowing entire camels—humps, hoofs, and lips included.[221]

- He noted the absurdity of worrying about a minuscule speck in someone else's eye, yet failing to notice the plank lodged in our own.[222]

- He cleverly portrayed the ridiculous notion of dead people digging graves for other dead people,[223] and the wanton tossing of valuable pearls to pigs.[224]

- He used comic exaggeration by describing a camel trying to squeeze through the eye of a needle.[225]

- He playfully and motivationally called Peter "The Rock," despite the fact that the impetuous fisherman was light years away from spiritual stability.[226]

While these examples may not leave you rolling in the aisles, they must have drawn some good laughs from the pig farmers and camel herders of Jesus' day. The Rabbi had a sharp sense of humor! If we deny this, we miss the significance of many of His statements.

An overly depressed perspective of Jesus, God the Son, will also affect our view of God the Father. The God who created intricate flowers, artistic sunrises, comically shaped fish, playful chimps, fat squirrels and dimples is not a dull, dour person. Nor does He want His sons and daughters to misrepresent Him before a world that so desperately needs to see Christians who are real, spontaneous and light-hearted—not sterile oddballs. Dull commentaries have drained the humorous life out of the lighter sides of Scripture. Yet it is God's Word that says, "...he who is of a merry heart has a continual feast."[227] Jesus laughed at life, and those who long to really live will learn to laugh with Him.

I LOVE MY LIFE

If we do not love the life God has given us, we have somewhere lost touch with the God who saved us. I am training my soul to wrap its arms around every second of my God-intended life. All days are equal. There is no best day in Heaven. Since before time began, a perfect God has flawlessly crafted every molecule, moment and memory.

The Father has heard and answered the prayers of Jesus, "Your kingdom come. Your will be done on earth as it is in Heaven."[228] As God loves and favors each of us equally, so He exercises His justice with absolute equity when writing scripts of identical value for His beloved children.

The greatest thing a leader can do is teach people how to live. This must include training others to love the life God has given them. Each day, I am learning how to love my vision for my life less, and God's vision for my life more. By loving God's plan for my life, I now love the only life worth living.

In John 12:25, Jesus challenges our shallow understanding of life: "He who loves his life *[Greek—is attached to his life]* will lose it, and he who hates his life in this world *[Greek—loves his life less]* will keep it for eternal life." If we are attached to our dream for our life, it will slip through our fingers. If, on the other hand, we embrace God's plan, whether we ever fully understand it or not, we will begin to live the pleasures of eternal life right now.

GOD DOESN'T WANT HIS SONS AND DAUGHTERS TO MISREPRESENT HIM BEFORE A WORLD THAT SO DESPERATELY NEEDS TO SEE CHRISTIANS WHO ARE REAL, SPONTANEOUS AND LIGHT-HEARTED—NOT STERILE ODDBALLS.

In this world, everyone experiences a measure of pleasure; everyone wins something! The devil is happy to give us the pleasures of Connecticut and Vermont Avenues, as long as he retains the pleasures of Boardwalk and Park Place. If you have ever played the board game Monopoly, you know Connecticut Avenue and Vermont Avenue are virtually worthless. By obtaining these properties you have won nothing of real value. You have peace, but not lasting peace. It is joy, just not real joy. It is pleasure, without eternity. Counterfeit intimacy—which I call *religion*—is a shallow substitute for a personal relationship with a God who is madly in love with us.

"Religion is the Opium of the People." Karl Marx was right—but for the wrong reasons. Religion does drug people into a fog of lifeless rituals. But Marx never understood the distinction between religion and relationship. If he had pushed beyond the meaningless ceremony and encountered the person of Jesus Christ, he would have found something far more dynamic and life changing than communism will ever be.

Lenin saw religion in a more utilitarian light: "We shall find our most fertile field for the infiltration of Marxism within the field of religion, because religious people are the most gullible and believe almost anything as long as it is clothed in religious language." Not only did he view religion as meaningless, but he looked down on its adherents as easy prey.

In this instance, communism is right on target. Religion has little to offer the world except a system of conscience-soothing routines. But the world doesn't need cosmetic surgery; it needs a heart transplant and only the power of Jesus Christ can perform that operation. Transformation must begin inside. Religion only powders the nose and colors the cheeks. A relationship with God Himself changes the heart first, and the rest follows naturally.

Real pleasure comes from real relationship, and you will never experience real pleasure until you get to know the only true God there is: the Lord Jesus Christ. Don't wait till you get to Heaven to experience the pleasures of knowing Him. You can enjoy His presence and His pleasure today in worship, in prayer, by washing your soul with God's Word, and by learning to be relationally connected with His family here on earth.

STOP BLAMING GOD FOR YOUR LIFE

Something is terribly wrong when we wish we had a different life; when we don't look forward to getting up in the morning; when we think our best days are behind us, and that past mistakes have disqualified us from having a great future. If we are rarely or never content, then we are not in love with the life God has intended for us. It is not that each of us grew up experiencing only bad things. What many of us experienced was the absence of good things. Before it is too late, you need to begin to live the wonderful life God purposefully designed for you.

Even if our external life changed, we would not necessarily respond differently to life. Initially we might, but in the end, we would all revert back to what we really believe. Our belief about life will always surpass our experience of life. We don't need to see more miracles; we need to respond properly to the ones surrounding us every day.

Jesus told the story of a rich man who died and was sent to hell. While there, he saw father Abraham in the distance and begged him to send someone to his five brothers to warn them of a similar fate. "Abraham said to him, 'They have Moses and the prophets; let them hear them.' And he *[the rich man in hell]* said, 'No, father Abraham; but if one goes to them from the dead, they will repent.' But he *[Abraham]* said to him, 'If they do not hear Moses and the prophets, neither will they be persuaded though one rise from the dead.' "[229]

If His contemporaries refused to believe the miracles of Jesus, why would anyone choose to believe our miracles? Such is the human condition. Unless someone experiences a dramatic inner transformation, his inner un-wholeness will taint his view of life. God has already done enough around me, now I need to let Him complete His work in me.

I am not waiting for God to answer my prayers. The purpose of prayer is not to get answers, but to get to know

SOMETHING IS TERRIBLY WRONG WHEN WE WISH WE HAD A DIFFERENT LIFE.

God! I am not waiting for God to heal my body. Every external miracle will eventually lead to unfulfillment if it does not turn our attention back to God. This is a great seduction. Only one-out-of-ten lepers came back to say thank you.[230] Each external desire will immediately be followed by another request: "If this or that would just happen... then I can be fulfilled." I used to be obsessed with what I did not have; I battled depression over what was not happening in my life. I will never go back to that mindset again. I was wasting both my time and God's.

THE PURPOSE OF PRAYER IS NOT TO GET ANSWERS, BUT TO GET TO KNOW GOD!

I once met a Christian man who had been the director of a psychiatric hospital for 25 years. I asked him what had surprised him most about people who are mentally ill. He said, "The fact that every patient I ever met was completely and utterly consumed with *Self*. It was Self in the morning, Self at noon, and Self at night." Focusing on Self is not the solution, it is at the very heart of the problem.

Oswald Chambers writes, "Anything that has even a hint of dejection spiritually is always wrong. If I am depressed or burdened, I am to blame, not God or anyone else. Dejection stems from one of two sources—I have either satisfied a lust or I have not had it satisfied. In either case, dejection is the result."[231]

When we each stand before the judgment seat of Christ,[232] replays of our lives will reveal that every thought, action, and intention from the heart of God was flawlessly designed for our good. At that most revealing of moments, we will each be completely and utterly without excuse.[233]

We must stop blaming God for our miserable lives, and begin to bless Him for the magnificent, daily opportunities He has given to each of us. When He truly becomes our Lord, life becomes lovely. Every moment, every breath all becomes a part of life's great adventure. As each thought is reigned in, they bow before a faultless God.[234]

Now is the time to surrender our hearts to Jesus as Lord! Now is the time to remove every excuse for not loving the life He has given us!

The psalmist wrote, "All my springs are in You."[235] The fresh water of life we are each thirsting for can only be found flowing from the throne of God.[236] The contaminated streams of this world will never satisfy. Jesus said, "...the Kingdom of God is within you."[237] In other words, either we have the kingdom of God in us or we do not have it at all. The kingdom of God is within me, if I will but look.

Jesus does not want to shut down your party. He wants to invite you to His. He has promised each of us, "If you believe in Me, come and drink! For the Scriptures declare that rivers of living water will flow out from within."[238] Even in the final verses of God's Word, He calls us to receive His abundant life, "The Spirit and the bride say, 'Come.' Let each one who hears them say, 'Come.' Let the thirsty ones come—anyone who wants to. Let them come and drink the water of life without charge."[239]

SUMMARY POINTS

- God does not give us overcoming life: He gives us life as we overcome.

- The doorway to our success is through our weakness.

- We don't need a new life, we need to appreciate the one God has given us.

- God has given us everything we need to love the life He has given us.

- God's will is that we would come to the place where we love the life He has given us, instead of wishing for what does not exist and would not satisfy us even if it did.

QUESTIONS FOR DISCUSSION

1. When thinking of a time when you really loved your life, what do you think made you feel that way? Have things changed for you? If so, how?

2. In the past weeks how have you chosen to love your life in challenging circumstances? Did you respond differently than you ordinarily would have in the past? Are there ways you could have responded better? What strategies could you implement that would help you respond better in the future?

3. Sometimes it's more difficult to love our lives when our friends and family are unable to love their own lives. How have your family and friends influenced your outlook? How have you seen God be faithful?

4. When are you most inclined to blame yourself? Blame God? Blame others? What is the benefit of blame? What is the drawback of blame?

5. What has God shown you about His character that motivates you to love your life? How has that impacted you?

RESTING IN THE
REALITY OF GOD

CHAPTER TEN

THERE'S NO BAD NEWS
IN GOD

The way to the prize is through the problems.
If we mistakenly take our eyes off of the prize,
eventually all we will see are our problems.

THE AFRICAN KING

There once was a king in Africa. He had a close friend who looked at life from a positive perspective. Whatever was transpiring, his friend would comment, "This is good!"

One day while the two friends were out hunting, the king gave his friend the responsibility of preparing and loading the guns. Yet somehow the friend made a mistake, for when the king fired a gun his thumb was blown off.

Immediately the friend made his characteristic response, "This is good!" The king was furious. He shouted, "No, this is *not* good," and immediately sent his friend to jail.

A year passed.

One day the king, while on another hunting expedition, went into a particularly dangerous region and was captured by a tribe of cannibals. The cannibals took him to their village, bound him to a spit, and prepared to make a fire beneath him. Yet just as they were beginning to light the wood, one of the cannibals noticed the king's missing thumb. A highly superstitious tribe, the cannibals refused to eat someone who was not completely whole. Instead of killing him, they untied the king and sent him away unharmed.

When the king returned home, he remembered how he had lost his thumb, and was saddened as he thought about the friend he had imprisoned.

Filled with remorse, the king went straight to the jail and told his friend what had happened with the cannibals, confessing to him, "You were right, it was good that my thumb was blown off. I am so sorry for putting you in jail for such a long time; it was a bad thing for me to do."

"No!" The friend once again responded. "This is good!" Startled, the king asked, "What do you mean, this is good? How could it be good that I sent you to jail for a year?"

The friend replied, "If you had not put me in jail, I would have been with you when you were captured by the cannibals, and they would have certainly killed and eaten me."

The friend's response to life demonstrates a marvelous principle. The same principle is found in Romans 8:28 when God promises every believer in Jesus Christ, "And we know all things work together for good to those who love God, to those who are the called according to His purpose."

Let's break this marvelous promise down:

"And we know"—not speculate or presume, but know with absolute certainty

"...all things"—not some or even most situations

"...work together for good"—our benefit

"...to those who love God"—more than anyone or anything else

"...to those who are the called according to His purpose"—not pursuing their own desires or ambitions, but pursuing God's

To sum up this biblical equation: "all things work for the good" for people who meet two qualifications:

1. they love God, and
2. they are called according to His purpose.

If you presently qualify for this wonderful promise from God, then rejoice and be diligent to train your soul to continuously trust in this warranty for life! If, on the other hand, you do not qualify for God's full coverage plan, there is still time to change your mind.

ETERNAL TIME TRAVELERS

When we completely love and are committed to the Lord, we are given the opportunity of fully embracing the reality that there is no bad news in God. Yet we will only see this if we train our eyes to see from a broader perspective than the daily grind. We must embrace a perspective that even transcends our lifetime here on earth. We must have eternity in our hearts[240] in order to accurately assess if our lives have truly worked for our good.

The Book of Hebrews offers a glimpse into the mindset of heroes of the faith who refused to let their past or present rob their future. Many godly men and women have left the planet having not seen all they hoped for. Yet in spite of this, these fathers and mothers of the faith were fully persuaded that their hopes and dreams would one day be fulfilled.

"These all died in faith, not having received the promises, but having seen them afar off were assured of them, embraced them and confessed that they were strangers and pilgrims on the earth. For those who say such things declare plainly that they seek a homeland. And truly if they had called to mind that country from which they had come out, they would have had opportunity to return. But now they desire a better, that is, a heavenly country. Therefore God is not ashamed to be called their God, for He has prepared a city for them." [241]

Recently, our church family took a trip to the Holy Land. The nation of Israel itself is a miracle; the land and its people had been separated for thousands of years, seemingly with no hope of ever being reunited. Yet, in 1948, against all odds, Israel once again became a nation. Since that time, there has been a remarkable restoration of this once desolate place. The Jewish homeland has been so restored it truly is a land flowing with milk and honey. [242]

The oceans of blessings poured out upon this once ravaged country are living proof that all things truly work for our good for those who love God and are committed to His purpose. As the Spirit of God prophesied in the Book of Amos, "I will bring back the captives of My people Israel; they shall build the waste cities and inhabit them; they shall plant vineyards and drink wine from them; they shall also make gardens and eat fruit from them." [243]

On our trip to Israel, I asked our Jewish tour guide if he thought God had been able to make something good out of the holocaust. He responded by saying, "...since one-third of all Jews worldwide were killed during that devastating period, their senseless death was certainly a catalyst to get the United Nations to support a resolution providing the Jewish survivors with a homeland." Once again, as in the case of the patriarch Joseph, what Satan meant for evil, God turned around for good. [244]

EMBRACING LIFE

There is only one way to follow God: by faith. Unless you walk by faith, one day you will find you are not following Him at all. It takes great faith to believe the promises of God more than our circumstances, but we each have been given enough faith to do so. Romans 12:3 assures us, "God has dealt to each one a measure of faith." Jesus adds, "...if you have faith as a mustard seed, you will say to this mountain, 'Move from here to there,' and it will move; and nothing will be impossible for you." [245]

What mountains of pain and discouragement are you facing? What mass of misery threatens to bankrupt your entire investment in God? John Osteen, the father of Joel Osteen, would often challenge his Houston, Texas congregation: "Stop telling God how big your mountains are, and start telling your mountains how big your God is."

I need the same amount of faith to embrace the life God gives me, as I needed to embrace the God who saved me. It takes no faith to say, "God has not given me a life worth loving." On the other hand, it takes great faith to believe the truth, "God can only give me a life worth loving." Like any good father, God gets far more glory out of us living fulfilled lives than unfulfilled lives; and unlike our earthly fathers, He is completely capable of making our fulfillment a reality. The primary problem we have is that we often fail to see our lives from God's point of view.

As we wade through a smorgasbord of life's circumstances, we must resist the temptation of rejoicing in only the opportunities that suit our fancy. The truly successful pilgrims of earth learned to eat the meals placed before them with grateful hearts. If we are not fully embracing the life God has given us, we have somewhere lost touch with the God who saved us. Oswald Chambers expresses it this way: "Until we can come face to face with the deepest, darkest fact of life without damaging our view of God's character, we do not yet know Him." [246]

In order to change the visible realm, you must learn to see into the invisible. The main goal in life is to see the eternal realities and not just the temporary distractions of earth. Our time here is a dress rehearsal for eternity. Every aspect of our life is a test. God will not give us new revelations of Himself until we are obedient to the revelations He has already given us. Therefore, if we mistakenly take our eyes off of the revelations we have already been given, eventually all we will see are our problems.

GOD WILL NOT GIVE US NEW REVELATIONS OF HIMSELF UNTIL WE ARE OBEDIENT TO THE REVELATIONS HE HAS ALREADY GIVEN US.

The more we get to know the perfect, completely captivating God, the more transformed our lives become. Truly living for Jesus should always bring greater satisfaction, not less. If we are not satisfied with the life He has given us, it is because we have our eyes focused on self and not on God. Only when we are fully satisfied with who He is will we at last be satisfied with the life He has purposed for us.

The closer we get to God, the more our understanding of perfection increases. As we grow in our knowledge of Him, we should feel increasingly less and less perfect—but it should not discourage us.

As we grow more attached to His perfection, we will be less stumbled by our own imperfection. The goal in life is not to measure up to God. That would be futile! Instead, the goal is to learn to rest so completely in His perfection that we are not overwhelmed by our own lack.

Most of the time, no one can hurt me more than I can hurt myself, and no one can bless me more than God.

LOOKING GOOD IN BAD LIGHTING

We will always look our best in bad lighting. Add some alcohol to the mix and even unattractive people look pretty good. On the other hand, if we want to really see how we look—we need to turn up the lights. Doctors' offices intentionally do not have bar room lighting and good doctors are never intoxicated when they examine patients. They want an accurate assessment of how their patients look; only more light can provide this.

There are occasions, however, when we are not necessarily looking for the most accurate representation of ourselves. Whenever our family goes to a professional photographer to get our picture taken, we don't care if the finished product is an exact representation of us. We'll take all of the help we can get in order to look our best.

Though a family portrait would be one of the few occasions we allow our self-image to be altered, it is impossible to imagine a doctor telling a patient, "I took a look at your x-ray and saw some significant abnormalities, but don't worry about it—I touched up the x-ray. Now it looks great!"

None of us would find comfort in someone attempting to alter reality in a life-threatening dimension. We all want our x-rays to be an accurate portrayal of what is really going on, because in this case unreality would destroy us. Don't mess with my x-rays!

So how does a perfect God relate to His imperfect creation without lowering His standard of perfection? John, the beloved apostle, affirms the purity of God when he writes, "...God is light and in Him is no darkness at all." [247] Just as the closer we get to good lighting the worse we look, the closer we get to God, the worse we look. That doesn't sound very exciting. Yet as we draw nearer to God we can see Him more clearly—and we can see He is smiling because of each of us. [248] What an incredible dichotomy! I'm looking worse and His smile is getting bigger. My value to Him has nothing to do with how I see myself, and is only based on how He sees me. He sees me clearly, and yet loves me dearly.

The satisfaction we are looking for will not come from God answering our prayers; it comes from learning to trust Him regardless of His answer. Therefore, the best response we can ever give to God is to smile back at Him.

God completes each of us, and that completion took place long before we were created. Jesus prayed, "Father, I desire that they also whom You gave Me may be with Me where I am, that they may behold My glory which You have given Me; for You loved Me before the foundation of the world." [249]

Just as the Father loved Jesus before the foundation of the world, He also loved us. [250] We are as loved by the Father as Jesus is, and that sacred romance began long before we even existed.

"Behold what manner of love the Father has bestowed on us, that we of all people should be called children of God!" [251]

THE UNTHINKABLES

An Australian missionary I once met spent years ministering to a South Pacific tribe without seeing any converts. One day, a member of the tribe accidentally electrocuted the missionary's nine-year-old son. The clan had a custom that when someone was killed, the victim's relatives had the right to take revenge on the person responsible for the death.

They expected the missionary to kill the one who had killed his son. But instead of exacting retribution, the missionary forgave his son's murderer. His response sent a shockwave through the tribe. They could not believe the missionary would not seek revenge.

Eventually, because of his selfless attitude, the entire tribe came to know Jesus. The missionary family had experienced an incomprehensible loss. However, because of their willingness to receive the grace of God, he and his wife were able to offer unthinkable forgiveness.

THE SATISFACTION WE ARE LOOKING FOR WILL NOT COME FROM GOD ANSWERING OUR PRAYERS; IT COMES FROM LEARNING TO TRUST HIM REGARDLESS OF HIS ANSWER.

Unthinkably challenging experiences are on the horizon for each of us. They will catch us totally by surprise and can shake us to our core. Most of the time they are events we thought would never happen—things that a loving God would never allow. And so when they occur we begin to question what we have never questioned before. How we respond to these unthinkable events in life will determine whether we become *bitter* or *better*.

Life is filled with the unthinkable. Businessmen don't start businesses because they want to experience bankruptcy. An athlete doesn't join a team because he's always wanted to sit on the bench. A politician doesn't run for an election hoping to lose. People don't get married because they plan on divorce.

HOW WE RESPOND TO THESE UNTHINKABLE EVENTS IN LIFE WILL DETERMINE WHETHER WE BECOME BITTER OR BETTER.

We don't mind the good unthinkables of life, like receiving an inheritance from a wealthy uncle you never met. But it's the seemingly bad unthinkables, like the sudden death of a loved one, chronic pain, or a terminal illness that rock our world. Yet, if we respond properly to the unthinkables, they can bring us to a whole new place of faith in our walk with God.

There were many unthinkables recorded in the Bible:

- Lucifer, the archangel, and one-third of the angels rebelled against God.

- Adam and Eve attempted to deceive God.

- Cain, the first-born son, killed his brother Abel.

- Jacob's older sons sold his beloved youngest son Joseph into slavery.

- Joseph revealed himself to his brothers as the second-in-command in Egypt, 20 years after they betrayed him.

- The children of Israel fell into full-blown idolatry while Moses was up on Mount Sinai receiving the Ten Commandments.

- Judas betrayed Jesus.

- Peter denied Jesus not just once, but three times.

Since the beginning of the world, unthinkables have happened. Yet, the Bible repeatedly shows that when someone goes through unthinkable trials with a proper attitude, God will grant him or her the grace to accept, and even thrive, in the situation.

Joseph, after being thrown into prison for fleeing from evil and clinging to what was good, maintained a good attitude toward both God and man. "...because the Lord was with him; and whatever he *[Joseph]* did, the Lord made it prosper." [252]

Job experienced an unthinkable loss when all of his ten children perished. That same day, all of his possessions were stolen and painful boils broke out over his body. Yet, he refused to curse God. Because he responded properly, God blessed the end of Job's life more than his beginning, giving him ten additional children and twice as many possessions. [253]

For years, King Saul chased David, and was intent on killing him. Yet, the promise of God to David remained steadfast, "...in everything *[David]* did he had great success, because the Lord was with him." [254]

Even Jesus experienced the greatest tests of His life when all of His disciples abandoned Him; when His mother watched Him die a gruesome death; and—the greatest unthinkable of all—when He lost fellowship with His Father by becoming sin for the whole world. Yet, here too, He conquered sin and death, and became "...the firstborn among many brethren."[255]

SUCCESS IS WHERE YOU FINISH

On November 6, 1986, Bob W. Ireland finished the New York City Marathon in 19,413th place. It was the slowest marathon time in history.

It might not have been a noteworthy event, except for the fact that Bob was the first person to run a marathon with his arms, instead of his legs. A 40-year-old California native, Bob had his legs blown off in Vietnam in 1969. Though it took him four days, two hours, 48 minutes, and 17 seconds, when asked why he ran the race, Bob, a born again Christian, said, "Success is not based on where you start, it's where you finish."

In the final book of the Bible, the Book of Revelation, the highest honor is given to one type of person: the Overcomer. Jesus Christ, the greatest Overcomer of all time, said, "He who overcomes, I will make him a pillar in the temple of My God, and he shall go out no more. I will write on him the name of My God and the name of the city of My God, the New Jerusalem, which comes down out of Heaven from My God. And I will write on him My new name."[256]

The true test of the overcoming life is being able to see that, in God, there truly is no bad news. The main issue is not our placement in the marathon of life, but rather what we had to overcome to place at all.

In 1994, my wife and I had the privilege of getting to know a dear family shortly after tragedy struck their lives. That year, Jan Cook experienced the jarring loss of both her husband of 30 years and her only son in a single-engine plane crash. The accident was neither her husband's or son's fault. Jan and her two grown daughters, Kathy and Chy, were left without a father and brother. It was an unthinkable event.

Though we had not met the Cook family prior to the crash, the reports of their deep family bond, and the courage of these three godly women, greatly impacted our lives. Each of them demonstrated an enormous resilience and dependency on Jesus that amazed us. Jan, for example, never missed teaching her weekly Bible study for 50 women.

Her unthinkable loss was met with unshakeable faith.

Now, 13 years since the accident, each of these godly women continue to trust the Lord for their lives and future. Recently, my wife and I had the privilege of having lunch with Jan, her daughter Kathy and son-in-law Bill. Jan shared with Suzie and me that about three years ago, God had asked her, "Jan, are you ready to thank Me for the life I have given you today, over the life that was taken away?" Jan, confessed it took her several days to answer. But she eventually told God, "Yes, Lord, I thank You for the life You have given me today over the life You have taken away."

All of us long to see Jesus in other people. It is always both humbling and inspiring.

Are these heroic responses to tragedy merely examples of extraordinary people, or are they, on the other hand, ordinary people who happened to respond well to the greatest tragedies in their lives? Even when they lacked faith, God remained faithful, because He could not deny His will and purpose for their lives.[257] I consider them heroes—they responded to life's greatest setbacks in a way I hope to follow.

When the major unthinkables come to rock your life, don't give up! Don't resign yourself to living an overwhelmed life. Jesus promised, "These things I have spoken to you, that in Me you may have peace. In the world you will have tribulation; but be of good cheer, I have overcome the world."[258] Jesus wants to give us peace in our pain, and joy throughout tribulations. If Jesus is a perpetual Overcomer, and "...my life is hid with Christ in God,"[259] then I'm called to be an overcomer as well.

Paul, the persecuted apostle, writes in the Book of Romans, "Who shall separate us from the love of Christ? Shall tribulation, or distress, or persecution, or famine, or nakedness, or peril, or sword? As it is written: 'For Your sake we are killed all day long; we are accounted as sheep for the slaughter.' Yet in all these things we are more than conquerors through Him who loved us."[260]

Though we are killed all day long, we are more than conquerors. Though, at times we may feel slaughtered by an onslaught of pressures and problems, we must always remind ourselves that the love Jesus has for us makes us victorious in each and every situation. There is no bad news in God!

RUNNING NAKED TO FREEDOM

One day, in Auschwitz, the infamous Nazi concentration camp, a Jewish inmate named Stanislaw Lec decided he could not take one more day in the nightmare around him. He made the decision to escape immediately, though he didn't know how. For weeks he would ask the other prisoners, "How can we escape this horrible place?" The answers he received always seemed the same, "Don't be a fool, there is no escape. Asking such questions will only torture your soul. Just work hard and pray you survive." Stanislaw refused to accept that answer and became obsessed with escaping.

One day, only a few feet from where he was working, he saw that a huge pile of bodies had been shoveled into the back of a truck. They were the bodies of men, women, and children who had been gassed. At the end of his workday Stanislaw ducked behind the truck. When no one was looking, he ripped off his clothes and dove, naked, into the pile of bodies. Pretending to be dead, he remained totally motionless for hours, even as more and more bodies were heaped on top of him. Stanislaw was nearly crushed with the weight.

THE LOVE JESUS HAS FOR US MAKES US VICTORIOUS IN EACH AND EVERY SITUATION.

The smell of rotting flesh and the rigid remains of the dead surrounding him were overwhelming. Yet he waited in stillness, hoping no one would notice him. Finally he heard the sound of the vehicle's engine starting and the truck began to drive away. After what seemed like an eternity, the truck stopped and dumped the corpses into a giant open grave. Completely still, Stanislaw remained buried under the corpses for hours until nightfall. When he finally felt certain no one was around, he removed himself from the mountain of cadavers, and ran, naked, 45 miles to freedom.

A man, in desperate need, was willing to lie in a pile of dead bodies for hours, and then run a marathon, naked, to freedom. Jesus was willing to die on a cross to rescue the whole world. He has told us, "a servant is not above his master nor is a student above his teacher."[261] As He has laid down His life for us, so we are called to lay down our lives for others.

Recently, the Holy Spirit spoke a word to my heart; it was

meant for me, as well as the congregation I serve. He challenged us, "If you stay where you are, you are going to die." It shook me! History has proved this true again and again, as unsuspecting masses have marched to their death—oblivious to the end.

Millions of Jews throughout Europe were gassed in Nazi concentration camps. During our trip to Israel, we visited the Holocaust Museum in Jerusalem. It was a life-changing experience. Over and over we listened to Holocaust survivors say that until the end they could not believe their lives would continue to get worse and eventually end in death. Each new horror they witnessed was met with disbelief. They simply could not believe human beings were capable of doing what they were seeing, and were continually shocked by each new atrocity.

A high-ranking Nazi leader once wrote concerning how six million Jews were able to be slaughtered, most without a fight, "The secret of our success was to keep the Jews deceived until the very last moment." It took the courage of a Stanislaw Lec to break free from the hypnotic deception surrounding him. Only then was he able to run 45 miles, totally naked, to freedom.

How about you? Are you willing to run naked to freedom?

Consider the life-threatening choices you are presently facing. Are you willing to acknowledge that Jesus was correct when He said that each of us are "...wretched, miserable, poor, blind, and naked?" [262]

Are you willing to leave the death and decay of this present world and run naked to Jesus, acknowledging the obvious, that "...all things are naked and open to the eyes of Him to whom we must give account?" [263]

While there is still time, will you humbly accept your increasingly desperate need for Jesus? As our Savior once told the Pharisees who were jealous that He had healed a blind man, "If you were blind, you would have no sin; but now you say, 'We see.' Therefore your sin remains." [264]

Lord Jesus, help us to always run away from what will certainly destroy us, and only toward what leads to everlasting life.

SUMMARY POINTS

- If we are not fully embracing the life God has given us, we have somewhere lost touch with the God who saved us.

- If we are not satisfied with the life He has given us, it is because we have our eyes focused on self and not on God. Only when we are fully satisfied with who He is will we at last be satisfied with the life He has purposed for us.

- The goal in life is not to measure up to God. That would be futile! Instead, the goal is to learn to rest so completely in God's perfection that we are not overwhelmed by our own lack.

- My value to God has nothing to do with how I see myself, and is only based on how He sees me.

QUESTIONS FOR DISCUSSION

1. Have you received news recently that you've interpreted as bad news? What do you think would change your thinking about this news? What are typical barriers to you changing your thinking? How do you think this affects you?

2. What are your typical responses to bad news? What are some ways that God is changing your response? How long does it usually take you to respond well? What strategies could you use to shorten your response time?

3. How do you define success for your life? What do you think would make you more successful? What do you think God's view of success is? How does your view and God's view of success compare?

4. As you have grown closer to God, how has your understanding of His view of you changed? How do you think your understanding of His view of you will change further? What parts of God's view of you are easiest for you to accept? What parts are hardest for you to accept? Explain.

5. What was most impacting on your life in this chapter regarding, "There's no bad news in God"? How did it affect your thoughts and feelings about bad news?

CHAPTER ELEVEN

THE END IS
THE PROCESS

SPIRITUAL WHIPLASH

Many years ago I was encouraged to read the classic daily devotional by Oswald Chambers, *My Utmost For His Highest*. Chambers had been a missionary to Egypt in the early part of the 20th century. Though he died in his mid-40s of appendicitis, he left a rich legacy of revelations for generations to come. Presidents of nations have read his devotional and leaned on the profound insights it provides.

Chamber's teachings were so weighty that at times I was shocked by his conclusions. I remember thinking there must have been been typos in the book, because some of what I read seemed so outlandish. In 1990, around the time I had received the rejection for my youth tour proposal, I read the following quote: "We must never put our dreams of success as God's purpose for us; His purpose may be exactly the opposite. We have an idea that God is leading us to a particular end, a desired goal; He is not. The question of getting to a particular end is a mere incident. What we call the process, God calls the end." [265]

What a concept! This quote dramatically changed the way I processed the will of God. Before receiving this revelation I had always believed God's goal for my life was for me to do great things for Him; it was the end result that really mattered. I hardly chewed my food; rarely smelled the flowers, and consequently never felt that what I had accomplished on any given day was good enough to meet the expectations of a perfect God. I was a man on a mission, with no time to waste. Constantly busy about my Father's business, but never believing I was fully capable of doing it. I figured I would rest when I arrived at where I was going. The problem was; I was so fickle I never arrived.

As I processed Chamber's quote, I realized God's primary goal was to transform my inner man to look like Him. He was far less concerned about the events in my life; His primary focus was my heart. I had been driven by an inner need for acceptance and self-worth, when God, having already completely accepted me, wanted to draw me by His Spirit.

If we refuse to embrace the process—every aspect of what we are going through—we will miss the entire point of life. In the Gospel of John, Jesus calls us to slow down and commune with Him. "I am the true vine, and My Father is the vinedresser. Every branch in Me that does not bear fruit He takes away; and every branch that bears fruit He prunes, that it may bear more fruit. Abide in Me, and I in you. As the branch cannot bare fruit of itself, unless it abides in the vine, neither can you, unless you abide in Me. I am the vine, you are the branches. He who abides in Me, and I in him, bears much fruit; for without Me you can do nothing." [266]

We live in an age where few know how to abide. Our culture trains us to spend our days rushing through life, preoccupied with outward accomplishment and having lost sight of the greater work God wants to do in each of us.

Growing up in New York City, life was a race. While driving, I learned early on, "he who hesitates is cut off" and "whoever gets there first is always right." I was so tightly wound, when I was just 15 years old, that I told a friend I didn't have time to enjoy a scenic view. He laughed, shaking his head in disbelief.

In John 15:1–2, Jesus was saying, in essence, "Stay plugged into Me and I'll empower your life; stay on the operating table, and you'll bear much fruit. But if you get off, all you'll have is a gaping hole and flying intestines."

Jesus emphasized this point in John 15:6–7, "If anyone does not abide in Me, he is cast out as a branch and is withered; and they gather them and throw them into the fire, and they are burned. If you abide in Me, and My words abide in you, you will ask what you desire, and it shall be done for you."

Clearly abiding is not optional in the Christian life. We are each given a graphic choice—abide and live, or wither and be thrown into the fire. The second part of verse seven is only true if we are doing the first part. Lots of people claim the right to "ask whatever you desire" but are not complying with "if you abide in Me and My words abide in you...." Asking whatever we desire is not a magic wand. It is contingent upon abiding in Jesus and allowing His words to abide *[Greek—dwell, endure, be present, remain]* in us.

Life is all about healthy growth that leads to bearing fruit; and the only way for that to happen is to dwell in the Author of life. "By this My Father is glorified, that you bear much fruit; so you will be My disciples." [267] Which makes parents happier: when their children succeed or when they fail? In the same way parents delight in their children and want them to succeed in life, God the Father is most glorified in us when we are most fruitful in Him. Though God's definitions of *success* and *failure* are different than ours, a continual, conscious dependence upon Jesus will always lead to healthy growth.

HEALTHY THINGS GROW

It is God's will for each of us to bear fruit. His power is extended to us so that with Him we can bear more fruit than we ever thought possible on our own. Plants are incredibly resilient. Just seeing a plant push its way through a crack in the cement shows us how strong they really are. In both the North and South Poles, there is moss that actually grows under the ice. God designed life to spring up even in the most unlikely places.

Though all healthy plants grow, not all growing plants are healthy for their environment. For years the southern United States has been battling a predator vine named kudzu. First introduced in 1876 at the Centennial Exposition in

ABIDING IS NOT OPTIONAL IN THE CHRISTIAN LIFE. WE ARE EACH GIVEN A GRAPHIC CHOICE— ABIDE AND LIVE, OR WITHER AND BE THROWN INTO THE FIRE.

Philadelphia, Pennsylvania, by the nation of Japan, kudzu was exhibited as an excellent ground cover. Yet in the exquisite soil of the American South, it became a ground cover on steroids.

Soon after planting kudzu, gardeners discovered the vine began to take over whatever was around it. Attractive and resilient, "the vine that ate the South" now covers over seven million acres, killing everything in its path. Kudzu can grow up to a foot a day during the peak summer months. Every year 60 feet of trees and even forests are smothered beneath its ravenous vines. In 1972, kudzu was declared a weed by the United States Department of Agriculture and continues to be a curse that cannot be stopped.

Sin is a kudzu in our lives. Though initially attractive, it soon grows out of control, consuming everything healthy: relationships, disciplines and destinies. Sin smothers our lives, blocking out the light of God's Word. "For you were once darkness, but now you are light in the Lord. Walk as children of light." [268] "For you have rescued me from death; You have kept my feet from slipping. So now I can walk in Your presence, O God, in your life-giving light." [269]

Abide in Jesus, the healthy Vine, and keep your heart from attaching itself to any parasite that will smother your life and destroy your future. Different people can be attracted to different parasites—inappropriate physical and emotional relationships, addictions, pornography, and bad attitudes. Whatever the seduction, "keep your heart with all diligence, for out of it spring the issues of life." [270]

If our end is growth at all costs, then MTV and the porn, drug and abortion industries are some of the healthiest things to ever hit planet Earth. Fortunately there is more to life than growth at all costs. While the enemy of life has come only to "...steal, kill and destroy," [271] true health is measured by the eternal value it brings to the people involved. Only what God authors can bear everlasting fruit; and the only way we can access eternal fruitfulness is by faith.

MORE LIGHT; MORE FRUIT

In Alaska, plants become dormant during the incredibly harsh winter season and remain suspended in an inactive state until the weather thaws. However, during the summer months, due to periods of 24-hour sunlight, plants can literally grow nonstop. Due to the constant sunlight, cabbages and other vegetables grow to an enormous size. Likewise, in

our lives the more light we allow to penetrate our darkness, the healthier we become. Yet, we can't spend our
entire lives in summer. We need the dormancy of winter,
the revitalization of spring and the transition of fall.

God is the God of all seasons. He is Lord of the process,
not just the end. In tropical climates, where plants have
longer growing seasons, jungles literally take over their
environment. With perfect temperature, enriched soil and
superabundant rainfall, the canopy of vitality provides
a natural greenhouse where everything thrives: plants,
insects, trees, and snakes. The environment is simultane-
ously lush and dangerous.

Sometimes when Christians have experienced a greenhouse environment, the dangers of fruitfulness become
self-evident. Jesus admonished, "Much is required from
those to whom much is given, and much more is required
from those to whom much more is given." [272] In the healthiest climates, everything grows faster—for the good and
the bad. "For a great and effective door has opened to
me, and there are many adversaries." [273]

DEAFENING SILENCE

Generally speaking, we hear the voice of God clearest in
winter. During the more fragrant and fruitful seasons of
our lives we are, frankly, too busy; too distracted. In winter, all we have is time. We've been rained-out, snowed-
under, or frozen solid. At last, God has our attention. If
we spend our time wishing winter was over, we will miss
the reason God created it in the first place—time to rest,
listen, and be restored.

Here again, Oswald Chambers provides some extraordinary insights. "When God gets us alone by affliction,
heartbreak, or temptation; by disappointment, sickness,

**GOD IS THE GOD
OF ALL SEASONS.
HE IS LORD OF THE
PROCESS, NOT JUST
THE END.**

or by a broken friendship; when He gets us absolutely alone, and we are dumbfounded, and cannot ask one question... then He begins to expound." [274]

IF YOU ARE QUESTIONING GOD ABOUT THE SEASON YOU ARE IN, YOU ARE NOT FULLY EMBRACING IT.

If you are questioning God about the season you are in, you are not fully embracing it. When God is in complete control of our lives we feel no need to ask Him questions. Questions indicate we have an agenda; that we think we know what should be happening in our lives. In short, questions indicate a lack of trust. Babies have no questions, only acceptance—complete trust, resting in their parent's arms. God wants to get us to a place where we are speechless, helpless and fully dependent upon Him. That kind of faith pleases Him the most. Jesus insisted, "Assuredly, I say to you, whoever does not receive the kingdom of God as a little child will by no means enter it." [275]

An unbelieving planet resists loudly, while the Kingdom of Faith persists quietly. Richard Wurmbrand, the Romanian pastor who spent 14 years in prison for his faith, once wrote, "The one thing you Americans are most afraid of is silence." How true. This is why fasting is so important. When we fast we finally get to listen without distraction. Perhaps, without the sound of chewing, we can hear God better.

When I fast, and by that I mean give up some pleasure for a season (e.g., food, entertainment, sports, desserts, etc.), I eliminate the distractions in my life so that I may fully focus on what is truly eternal. I quiet my soul to hear the voice of God. I don't fast because I think I'm hyperspiritual; I fast because I know I'm not. Fasting doesn't bring out the best in me; it exposes the worst. Spiritual toxins bloat and constipate my relationship with God. It is only when I allow the Spirit and the Word to wash over my soul that I am cleansed from the distractions of life.

Life tends to make us calloused. Fasting softens and humbles us. It forces us to see ourselves as we really are—frail and needy. Paul the apostle admitted he needed to fast often. [276] In Matthew 4, Jesus was led by the Holy Spirit to go into the wilderness to be tempted by Satan. He fasted 40 days and nights. Then "...the tempter came to Him, he said, 'If You are the Son of God, command that these stones become bread.' But Jesus answered and said, 'It is written, "Man shall not live by bread alone, but by every word that proceeds from the mouth of God.' " [277] Jesus needed the humility of fasting to activate the raw power of the Word of God. Masses of humanity gorge themselves on the crumbs of Earth; not realizing their true hunger is for the feasts of Heaven.

The earth is filled with people "...whose end is destruction, whose god is their belly, and whose glory is in their shame—who set their mind on earthly things." [278] Many years ago, when safes had rotary combination locks, thieves would use their fingers as hypersensitive listening devices. The most astute safecrackers would file the calluses off their fingertips in order to become more sensitive to the slightest gyrations of the lock. In fasting, we file away the hardness of life, in order to hear the still, small voice of our Creator. When we fast, we are encased in the process of getting to know God. Distractions are starved out; true feasting begins. Jesus told His startled disciples, "I have food to eat of which you do not know," [279] and "My food is to do the will of Him who sent Me, and to finish His work." [280] Come and dine; the Master's calling.

WE WERE ONCE DARKNESS

Though many of us have at times been afraid of the dark, darkness was the very first season the creation experienced. "In the beginning God created Heaven and earth. Now the earth was formless and empty, darkness was over the surface of the deep, and the Spirit of God was hovering over the waters." [281]

In the beginning of all things there was darkness; [282] but darkness, by its very nature, is insatiable. It is the gnawing repetition of darkness that makes us crave the light. No one ever ended their life wishing they had given themselves over to greater darkness. The opposite is true. When I gave my life to Jesus, I was so sick of the darkness I wanted to end my life.

I'm still sick of darkness.

Solomon illustrated this principle when he wrote, "Honey seems tasteless to a person who is full, but even bitter food tastes sweet to the hungry." [283] I can remember many nights during my life when I couldn't wait for the night to be over and morning to come. Every day, people frantically long for their night of desperation to be over and a day of hope to dawn at last.

Each day is likewise a microcosm of the four seasons. It begins in darkness, nighttime (12:01 AM), often, the coldest part of the day. Metaphorically speaking, we launch our day in winter. Gradually, the morning warms up, and we enter a type of springtime. During the heat of the day, we experience a mini-summer; and as the sun sets, and it starts to cool off, we enter fall.

All of our lives start out in darkness: both natural and spiritual. Yet though we all have the option of moving into the light, most people on the planet are still in darkness. "If we say that we have fellowship with Him, and walk in darkness, we lie and do not practice the truth." [284] "This is the crisis we're in: God-light streamed into the world, but men and women everywhere ran for the darkness. They went for the darkness because they were not really interested in pleasing God." [285]

Men love darkness; yet God still loves men.

As John Newton, the author of the famous Christian hymn *Amazing Grace,* wrote, "I once was blind, but now I see." If we have been born again, we are now called to walk in the light. "For you were once darkness, but now are you light in the Lord. Live as children of light." [286] One of the greatest miracles I have ever seen has taken place in my own heart. I, who once loved darkness, now love light. If there is a greater miracle than that, I have never seen it.

GOD FOR ALL SEASONS

If you don't know the season your life is in, you will have a really hard time. If you are look-ing for fruit on your tree in the middle of winter, you are going to be disappointed. If you are trying to hold on to parts of your life in the fall, when emotional leaves are falling away, you will be very frustrated. It is a waste of time to pine for springtime in winter, lust for summer in spring, and long for fall in summer. The fruit of each season is designed to bring us closer to Jesus so He can bring healing to our lives. [287]

When God wants spring to come in your life, it will happen. But we do ourselves a distinct disservice by refusing to embrace what is right in front of us. Spring flowers will come soon enough. In the meantime, don't miss what God is trying to show you today. *The Message Bible* says it quite well: "Give your entire attention to what God is doing right now, and don't get worked up about what may or may not happen tomorrow. God will help you deal with whatever hard things come up when the time comes." [288] I have wasted too many wonderful days, in magnificent places, with fascinating people, because I was unable to get my heart around what was happening, and instead longed for what was not. I will never get those days back, but I am committed to relearn what I missed then.

There is no best season in life. When I received Jesus as my Lord and Savior, it was a springtime experience. I was so high I thought I would never come down. Then came a seemingly endless summer when all kinds of fruit surfaced in my life. But when, in time, fall arrived and I lost the warm fuzzies, I got really discouraged.

Once-healthy leaves were falling off every dimension of my life. I desperately longed for spring and summer again, but things only seemed to get worse. Instead of being revital- ized, I felt more and more dead. My heart was frozen in the winter of my discontent. I whined, squawked, and begged God to restore what once was. But He had no interest in playing reruns; He had brand-new dimensions of character He wanted to reveal in me. He was committed to conforming me to His own image: the God of ALL seasons. As a loving Father, He refused to yield to my naïve complaints. In the end, spring did return, but the cycle of life and death would be revisited over and over throughout my life.

Our best season in life should be the one we are presently in. Some people hate winter, when everything they were attached to lies dead at their feet. But everyone goes through winter.

Initially, as a young Christian, all I longed for were the springtime and summer experi- ences in God. Over time, however, I realized every season has its pitfalls. King David was seduced in the spring [289] and Adam and Eve had their great fall during the summer. [290]

I began to realize that during prolonged fall and winter seasons, God was able to do a much deeper work in me than He was through the flowers of spring and fruit of summer. I learned to embrace the dying of fall, as once flourishing dimensions of my life seemed to wither and drop off. These desperate seasons provoked me to become more attached to God and less to what I thought I needed from Him. It was during my spiritual winters, when my life appeared dead and frozen, that God performed the deepest internal transformation within my soul and spirit. I would not trade the profound work God has done in me for life in an easier season.

IT WAS DURING MY SPIRITUAL WINTERS, WHEN MY LIFE APPEARED DEAD AND FROZEN, THAT GOD PERFORMED THE DEEPEST INTERNAL TRANSFORMATION WITHIN MY SOUL AND SPIRIT.

The first disciples started out their spiritual walk in springtime. It seemed that following Jesus made everything better. Around the time Jesus raised Lazarus from the dead, Christ's ministry was peaking. "If He can raise people from the dead," His disciples thought, "He could liberate us from Rome." In the history of the world, the notion that Christ's goal was in some way tied to liberating his followers from Rome has to be one of the most serious under-assessments of a person's potential ever recorded. They didn't realize until after He was dead that Christ's greater goal was to liberate them from something far more dangerous than the Roman Empire—themselves. The enemy within was a greater threat to their purpose and destiny than all of the oppression of Rome.

Soon after Jesus raised Lazarus from the dead, He told His disciples He was leaving. His disciples freaked out saying, "Lord, you don't understand. We're booked. We've got overflow crowds, the TV networks are lining up... you could run for Prime Minister!" Jesus shrugged; He knew that winter was coming, and the sellout crowds were about to shrivel. After the crucifixion, the multitudes dwindled from multiplied thousands to everyone fleeing; from 500 people who personally saw the resurrected Jesus, to 120 people in an upper prayer room, praying once again for spring.

We must know the season we are in, in order to receive the full benefit of God's perfect plan. "The stork knows the time of her migration, as do the turtledove, the swallow, and the crane. They all return at the proper time each year. But not my people! They do not know what the Lord requires of them." [291]

Peter, not knowing the season he was in, made promises to Jesus he couldn't keep. "Lord, why can I not follow You now? I will lay down my life for Your sake." Jesus answered him, "Will you lay down your life for My sake? Most assuredly, I say to you, the rooster shall not crow till you have denied Me three times." [292] How can I embrace a season if I insist on denying I am in it? Once again, I have to know where I am in order to get where I need to go.

Oswald Chambers wrote, "There never has been a saint yet who did not have to live a maimed life to start with." [293] How many of you have always dreamed of living a maimed life?

"How was your day, honey?"

"Oh, it was pretty...maimed."

"That's nice, dear! Can you take out the garbage?"

Never trust a man without a limp. Never trust someone who does not demonstrate his desperate need to be dependent upon God. His false sense of security only means he has not been sufficiently tempered by the seasons of life. Do not give significant responsibility to people who have not been tested by fire, for when their lives heat up, like chocolate soldiers, they will melt.[294]

Most of all: do not trust yourself. When you realize you are not walking with a limp, fall to your knees. Let Jesus prune you! Let Him trim off what is dead and stinking. Let Him remove what has no lasting value and will only weigh you down. Soon you will rebound from your winter, basking among the beautiful flowers and sweet fruit of a fully surrendered life, reflecting on how wonderful your winter was—no longer dreading fall and winter's return.

FRUIT IS NOT OPTIONAL

Jesus admonished, "I am the true vine, and My Father is the vinedresser. Every branch in Me that does not bear fruit He takes away; and every branch that bears fruit He prunes, that it may bear more fruit." [295] Every challenge God sends our way is designed to make us more fruitful. He removes areas in our lives we have been attached to, some of which are now dead. Though they may have previously been highly fruitful, they are now a hindrance to our future growth.

God is not enamored by how we look on Earth. As a wise Father, He is committed to firmly establishing our internal, long-term health. Therefore, He cuts away what we are attached to, even what appears to be healthy, in order to produce His destiny for our lives.

Pruning is not hacking; it is precision trimming. Though a significant pruning may look pretty ugly, like any fresh haircut, "...nevertheless, afterward it yields the peaceable fruit of righteousness to those who have been trained by it." [296] In nature, depending upon the species of plant or tree, pruning can take place during any season of the year, especially when cutting away dead branches.

So, what is the value of God pruning our lives?

1. **Pruning exposes unseen areas in our life to air and light.** Dimensions that have been obscured and hidden are brought to the forefront and given a measure of prominence.

2. **Pruning corrects and repairs damaged branches in our life that have died for unknown causes.** Dead branches should be removed as soon as we see them. If they are diseased, pruning will keep the infection from spreading to healthy areas in our life. After sinning with Bathsheba, King David wrote, "Behold, You desire truth in the inward parts, and in the hidden part You will make me to know wisdom." [297]

3. **Pruning encourages flowers and fruit to come forth.** Flowers soon become fruit, allowing the seeds contained within the fruit to produce new life. Pruning brings forth a beauty that can only be revealed as we die to ourselves.

4. **Pruning directs and controls future growth.** When we trim off side branches, we encourage growth in the main trunk. So often in life we give our energy to dead branches that drain us and keep us from growing in other areas. If we wait too long to trim off dead branches there can be extensive injury to the trunk. "...purge out the old leaven, that you may be a new lump...." [298] These draining branches, are called "suckers" and can be anything from relationships, friend-ships., bondages, entertainment to addictive behaviors.

5. **Pruning is necessary after we have gone through a significant transplanting in our lives.** The very nature of transplanting means roots (i.e., relationships, areas of ministry, even resources) will be severed. Therefore, a tree's branches should be trimmed in direct proportion to the number of roots that have been cut. Even though transplanting is by its very nature painful, we must learn to embrace the pruning that follows.

6. **Pruning rectifies bad judgment.** At times, a planter will mistakenly place a tree in a spot that it will eventually outgrow. Thus the challenge to leaders: replant those under our care so that they can grow to their full size in larger pots.

7. **Pruning is essential in order to lessen the damage a tree will experience during storms.** I have seen leaders who seemed to have big, fruitful trees. Yet, beneath the surface lay rotten dimensions in their lives they refused to allow God to prune. Eventually, the large infected branches they were attached to broke off, taking part of the trunk with them. What could have been corrected in its infancy became a life-threatening travesty.

8. **When God is at work in our lives, He prunes!** When it is large, He uses bulldozers. Sometimes it's radical! But do not fear; in time, old fruit orchards are pulled up and new ones planted. All for the good! For a few short years you will not see the fruit you once did. But get ready, in God's perfect time your harvest will be abundant.

Let me sum this chapter up:

> If you find yourself enjoying the fruit of summer—be grateful.
> If God is calling you to enter the embrace and separation of fall—rejoice.
> If you are immersed in the external dormancy of winter—thank God every day.
> If the first buds of spring are sprouting in your life—be greatly encouraged.

The purpose of life is to learn from the process. There is no best season, no magic moment. God has called us to overcome in every season. As I have grown in my relationship with Jesus, I have become increasingly more indifferent to the season I am in. Each is ordained by God; having an eternal, lasting value, if I can but see them through the eyes of a loving Creator.

SUMMARY POINTS

- If we refuse to embrace the process—every aspect of what we are going through—we will miss the entire point of life.

- Life is all about healthy growth that leads to bearing fruit; and the only way for that to happen is to dwell in the Author of life.

- Only what God authors can bear everlasting fruit; and the only way we can access eternal fruitfulness is by faith.

- If you are questioning God about the season you are in, you are not fully embracing it. When God is in complete control of our lives, we feel no need to ask Him questions. Our best season in life should be the one we are presently in.

QUESTIONS FOR DISCUSSION

1. Think of a recent situation when you hurried to get to the end. How did the end benefit you? How did the process benefit you? What part do you tend to focus on more? Why?

2. Think of a Kudzu in your life. What areas of health is it strangling out? How would removing it from your life benefit you? How would it hurt you? Has God given you a strategy for dealing with you Kudzu? If you do that, what do you think would happen?

3. What spiritual season of your life has had the greatest short term benefit for you: spring, summer, fall, or winter? Which spiritual season had the greatest long term benefit? What season are you currently in? How is God using it to bring fruit forth in your life?

4. What areas of your life is God pruning right now? How do you feel about God's pruning? What has God's pruning revealed to you? What are some strategies that God has given you for growth in this new season?

5. Do you regularly take the time to rest, listen, and be restored? How does this affect your life?

CHAPTER TWELVE

PERFECTLY POSITIONED
FOR THE REST OF YOUR LIFE

OBSTACLES ARE OPPORTUNITIES IN DISGUISE

Every irritation is an invitation to go to the next level.

Frustrations are veiled doorways to our destiny. Until we see our lives from God's point of view, we will never see the good that is possible because of these frustrations. If we obsess over the pain and displeasure inherently associated with the struggles of life, we will miss the entire point. Each of our lives are intentionally shrouded in secrecy; our true purpose disguised in a maze of problems. Complaining about the setbacks only distracts us from receiving the truth behind the mystery. The key to life is to not stop at the surface of a problem, but to dig deep enough to uncover the reason and value behind each trouble.

One night, many years ago, I had the privilege of leading my wife's mother to Jesus. My father-in-law had gone to bed hours before, but God led me to stay up and talk to Suzie's mom about her relationship with God.

Around midnight, after an hour of challenging her about the fragile condition of her soul, Mom invited Jesus back into her life. She had been backslidden for over 50 years. Suzie's grandmother's prayers had finally caught up with her wayward daughter. Mom had seen her daughter Suzie, and her two sons and both of their wives, come to know Jesus. Their changed lives affected her, and she gave her heart wholly to Him. It would be a few more years before Dad threw in the towel and turned his life over to God as well.

A short time after Mom made her recommitment, Suzie and I were sitting around her kitchen table talking with her about God. Dad was not home. Just as we joined hands to pray, the phone rang. Mom stopped to answer it, said hello, and listened for only a few seconds before putting the phone down, stunned. It was an obscene phone call. Annoyed and offended by this assault against my mother-in-law and the attempt to distract our time of prayer, I grabbed the phone and began to listen.

The man on the other end was shouting every foul word you can imagine. As he continued to yell, I decided to yell back, "I KNOW WHY YOU'RE CALLING! YOU'RE A LONELY, MISER-ABLE MAN, BUT GOD WANTS TO SET YOU FREE! THAT'S WHY YOU CALLED THIS NUMBER! JESUS LOVES YOU AND WANTS TO RELEASE YOU FROM THE BONDAGES IN YOUR LIFE..." and on and on. After about 45 seconds of passionately preaching, I realize he had stopped yelling and cursing and was actually listening. Finishing my mini-sermon, I blurted out, "So, what do you think?" After a few seconds of silence, I heard a quivering voice answer, "I think you're right."

That opened an astounding door. We quickly began to talk about his life. It turned out the caller was a 19-year-old backslidden Christian who was obviously far away from God. I was able to talk and pray with him for 20 minutes or so, assuring him that both Jesus and I had forgiven him; even offering to meet with him to help him sort out his life. Though he was probably too embarrassed to take me up on my offer to meet face to face, I am convinced that phone call significantly impacted his life.

There are no coincidences in God, only opportunities.

Though the obscene caller may have thought it was just a phone call, God had a greater plan—He turned that phone call into a lifeline to save this young man's soul. "For he has rescued us from the one who rules in the kingdom of darkness, and he has brought us into the Kingdom of his dear Son."[299]

From this moment on, let your default attitude be, "God, what marvelous thing are You trying to show me through the challenges I am presently facing? I believe they are working for my good, and will produce the '...peaceable fruit of righteousness,' if I respond well."[300]

Though Paul the Apostle was in prison and would eventually be beheaded, he still saw how God graciously used for good what Satan meant for evil. Refusing to see his circumstance in a negative light, Paul wrote, "Now I want you to know and continue to rest assured, brethren, that what *[has happened]* to me *[this imprisonment]* has actually only served to advance and give a renewed impetus to the *[spreading of the]* good news *[the gospel]*."[301] His positive response to adversity became a doorway of opportunity to reach an unreached people group—the prison inmates and guards in Caesar's Palace.

In 1962, Victor and Mildred Goertzel published a revealing study of 413 famous and exceptionally gifted people, called *Cradles of Eminence*. The couple spent years attempting to understand what produced such greatness; what common thread might run through all of these extraordinary people's lives.

Surprisingly, the most outstanding fact was that virtually all of them, 392 out of 413, had to overcome very difficult obstacles in their lives in order to become who they were. The difficulties in our lives are the greatest shapers of our destinies.

PERFECTLY POSITIONED FOR THE REST OF YOUR LIFE

Absolutely everything we have gone through in life has prepared us for the God-conceived opportunities and challenges ahead. Pedigrees of divine intention extend both backward and forward, connecting every seemingly random situation with the redemptive purposes of God.

When my family and I lived in Los Angeles, our then-14-year-old daughters were invited to a slumber party with some of their friends. We were told to drop our girls off at 11:00PM, despite the fact that the party was in a very rough part of town. When my wife and I arrived at the dimly lit street, we immediately began to assess our surroundings.

As we looked down the empty street, we could faintly see four silhouettes fanned out across the road. They were spaced apart and walking toward us at a slow, menacing pace. Though the girls were anxious to see their friends, I told them to wait, lock their doors, and stay in the car.

The four figures came closer to our vehicle. They were clearly members of a gang. But instead of passing us by, one guy, the largest one of the group, walked to the rear of our car and stood facing us. He folded his arms stiffly together, staring us down.

We froze. For at least a full minute no one spoke or moved. Finally, feeling the need to do something, I decided to get out of the car to talk with him. I reached for the door and unlocked it, but when I tried to pull on the door's handle, nothing happened. Click. Click. Click. Still nothing. I tried to lock and unlock the door repeatedly, but it would not open. I could still see the young man standing behind our vehicle, and I knew he could hear my pathetic attempts to open it. In an awkward kind of way, it was embarrassing. I couldn't even open my own car door.

Finally, I watched him angrily unfold his arms and wave his hands at me in disgust. He turned and walked away, rejoining his friends. When they were out of sight, I had one of my daughters get out of the back seat and let me out. I walked the girls to the house and then my wife and I drove away.

Yet my door, which had worked flawlessly until that moment, still would not open. A few days later, I invited a mechanically-inclined friend over to my house, and we took the inside of the door off. What he showed me was startling. The inner workings of the door had not broken. As impossible as it may seem, the two connected parts just separated. We both agreed, in the natural it couldn't have happened; yet it did. Jesus said, "What is impossible from a human perspective is possible with God."[302]

Hindsight is 20/20. In retrospect, I don't think the gang member wanted to chat or have a Bible study. I believe my decision to get out of the car was a bad idea and God protected my life. Most likely I (and perhaps even my family) would have been seriously harmed. My Father in Heaven had miraculously intervened. It is a vivid demonstration of how He watches over every aspect of our lives. "He will not let you stumble and fall; the One who watches over you will not sleep."[303]

It was God's will to show Himself strong on my behalf. I was perfectly positioned to see the miraculous hand of God and I didn't even know it. We are each continually positioned for success. All that is needed is for our hearts to remain open and trusting, surrendered to the One greater than our meager little plans.

As Paul the Apostle urged, "I pray that your hearts will be flooded with light so that you can understand the wonderful future He has promised to those He called. I want you to realize what a rich and glorious inheritance He has given to His people."[304]

FACE YOUR FEARS

Every day people perish for lack of understanding,[305] living so much less than God intended. I once read about a young girl who spent 87 days in a row eating her lunch in a bathroom stall at school because she felt so insecure and rejected.

I can relate. During my pre-adolescent years, while living in the strict, all-boys boarding school, we would take daily, mandatory showers in a large, open room. Much to my personal embarrassment, it was obvious to all that I was one of the last to develop body hair. I felt completely inadequate and worthless. With no one to talk with about the issue, I solved the problem by spending months hiding in a bathroom stall during evening shower time. In order to appear as if I had taken a shower, I would put water in my soap dish, and then sprinkle it over my head before exiting the stall.

On a few occasions, I remember the sick feeling of thinking I had been caught, though I never was. Even as I write this, some 45 years later, I still feel the excruciating humiliation of this youthful trial. If only my story were unfamiliar to the human condition. But mankind has been prone to hide since the Garden of Eden.[306] Why do we hide from the God who loves us, and from the divinely orchestrated events designed for our maturing and growth? If we face our fears, they will dissolve. If we bow down to them, they become bondages, strongholds, and even generational curses.

Three weeks before Christmas in 1993, a 43-year-old man in Berlin, Germany, died while watching TV. No one noticed he was gone. His rent continued to be paid, automatically, out of his bank account. Five years later, when his money had finally run out, his landlord entered his apartment to see what had happened. He found the man's remains in front of his TV. The TV Guide was opened on his lap to December 3, 1993, the presumed day of his death. Although the television set had long since burned out, the lights on his Christmas tree were still twinkling away. What a grim finale to a forgotten life.

I hope someone notices when I die. I hope that my presence will in some way be missed. I hope I live such a life of caring for others, that at my point of need someone cares for me. May we never give up on God or people. May our hearts and minds remain steadfastly open to see our lives as God intended. May we always believe that our best days are always ahead.

I know even when I feel overlooked by others, I am never invisible to God. Jesus has promised each of us that our Father in Heaven is aware of all our needs. "Are not two sparrows sold for a copper coin? And not one of them falls to the ground apart from your Father's will. But the very hairs of your head are all numbered. Do not fear therefore; you are of more value than many sparrows."[307] We must continually remind ourselves how invaluable, even priceless, we are to our heavenly Father. Behind every challenging circumstance, there is a loving God whose victorious perspective is far greater than the trial we face.

WHO'S HOLDING YOUR ROPE?

Many years ago, there was a fishing village next to a turbulent river. One day a boy fell into the river. A crowd quickly gathered. A rope was brought, and the strongest swimmer in the village volunteered to rescue the boy. He tied one end of the rope around his waist, threw the other end to the crowd and jumped into the river.

The crowd watched him swim through the violent current to reach the terrified child. When he finally grabbed a hold of the boy, the crowd cheered and people began to yell, "Pull in the rope!" As the villagers looked at one another, someone shouted, "Who's holding the rope?" No one was holding the rope. In the excitement of watching the rescue, the crowd had let the end of the rope slip into the water. Powerless to help, all they could do was watch the boy and his would-be rescuer sink beneath the devouring waters and drown.

Who's holding the rope in your own life? Who's healing your past? Who's sustaining your present? Who's securing your future? Decide now. Tomorrow may be too late. Don't learn how to box when you are fighting for your life. Don't figure out how to fire your gun when the thief is coming through your bedroom window. Fight for your life now! Don't postpone living for a tomorrow that may never come. Jesus challenged us, "Therefore do not worry about tomorrow, for tomorrow will worry about its own things. Sufficient for the day is its own trouble."[308]

"Whatever happens, dear brothers and sisters, may the Lord give you joy. I never get tired of telling you this. I am doing this for your own good. I don't mean to say that I have already achieved these things or that I have already reached perfection! But I keep working toward that day when I will finally be all that Christ Jesus saved me for and wants me to be."[309]

If you are bored, it is not God's fault. Boredom is a result of being unable or unwilling to see life from God's perspective. The God who made galaxies isn't boring. If we say we are following God, and yet lack the passion and purpose He intended, then we have somewhere along the way lost touch with who He really is. Without knowing who He is, we can never realize who we are.

Recently, our missions pastor at The Rock of Roseville, Marco Prado, challenged our church family, "How many adventure movies do we have to watch before we begin to live the adventure God has planned for us?" Every second we have spent wishing we were *somewhere* else, or perhaps even that we actually were *someone* else, has been a tragic waste of time, and a slap in the face of a God who has done everything possible for our well-being. We must stop waiting to live and start living. Our God-given opportunities are quickly slipping through our fingers. Like a comet that passes but once, our lives are gliding by ever so quickly, never to return. Unless we open our eyes, we will miss parts of life we will never see again.

EFFORTLESS FAITH
Contrary to most people's misconceptions, faith requires no effort whatsoever—faith only requires surrender. True faith is effortless; like ripened fruit, it falls into our hands with ease. Jesus promised, "For My yoke is easy and My burden is light."[310] A partial faith in God is really distrusting Him. In the same way a hospital patient, about to be operated on, must fully submit to the will of the attending health professionals, completely trusting the judgments and decisions that are beyond his or her control, we must likewise trust God by fully submitting to His will for our lives.

EVERY SECOND WE HAVE SPENT WISHING WE WERE SOMEWHERE ELSE, OR PERHAPS EVEN THAT WE ACTUALLY WERE SOMEONE ELSE, IS A SLAP IN THE FACE OF GOD.

God has not brought you this far to fail, but to finish well. Paul the Apostle was "...confident of this very thing, that He who has begun a good work in you will complete it until the day of Jesus Christ...."[311] God will finish what He has started in us, and we will be more than just pleased, we will be amazed! If we yield to His plan for us, God promises our lives will be, "...exceedingly abundantly above all that we ask or think, according to the power that works in us...."[312]

We don't need God to do one more thing for us. What He has previously done and is presently doing is more than sufficient. He doesn't have to demonstrate even one more time His love and care for my life. He has done enough. If we can just remember; if we can keep spiritual amnesia from overtaking our shallow consciousness, then we are set for life. In our right minds, we will overflow with gratitude. With a proper view of the panorama of our lives, the only appropriate response to a loving God is, "Thank You," a million times over. We should be increasingly more and more grateful to a generous Creator who has fashioned, flawlessly, every dimension of our lives.

FROM THE UTTERMOST
Years ago, Suzie, the girls and I toured New Zealand with Trevor Yaxley. The last concert on the nine-city tour was in Invercargill, the southernmost city in that island nation. As you enter the city there is a sign that reads, "Welcome to Invercargill, New Zealand—The Uttermost Part of the Earth." Apparently, Invercargill is the furthest city from Jerusalem on Earth. It was a peculiar sign and made a distinct impression on me when I saw it. The expression "uttermost part of the earth" is taken from Acts 1:8 in the King James Version of the Bible. "But ye shall receive power, after that the Holy Ghost is come upon you: and ye shall be witnesses unto me both in Jerusalem, and in all Judea, and in Samaria, and unto *the uttermost part of the earth [emphasis mine]*."

The complete impact of the sign did not hit me until a few days later, when we were about to fly out of the country from Invercargill. I had been working on an intense creative project, and was saddened that I had not been able to meet and dialogue about the project with a friend and advisor, Winkie Pratney. At that time, Winkie and his family would spend half the year living in the U.S. and the other half in his hometown of Auckland. We had been with them in both places, and I had looked forward to being together again. Though I had tried to get ahold of him, I could never reach him.

As we were sitting on the 30-seat plane loading passengers, I sat disappointed that I had missed seeing Winkie. Just as this thought crossed my mind, Winkie walked onto the plane. We were shocked to see each other! Only God could have orchestrated that meeting. We then spent the next two hours, as we flew to Auckland, catching up on our personal lives and discussing the project. His advice, as always, was just what I needed. I was amazed by the sovereignty of God in this situation. As I reflected on it, God spoke to my heart, "I can meet your needs from the uttermost parts of the earth." Time and again, He has proven Himself more than faithful to affirm this promise.

ADVENTURES OR DISASTERS?

Many of us have had experiences in which we came within a whisker of losing our lives. At times, our brush with death so terrified us it became a memory we would rather forget. Several years ago I traveled to Italy to visit my sister and her family. My nephew picked me up at the airport in Rome. From there, it was a four-hour drive to my sister's home in southern Italy. I was completely exhausted, and began to doze off as he navigated the rain-soaked roads.

As we exited the highway, on the final stage of the journey, he took a 90-degree turn much too fast. The streets were slick and there was nothing that could be done. As my nephew shouted, "We're going over!" I cried out, "Jesus, help us!" We catapulted over a 30-foot cliff, and began to tumble end-over-end. I had no idea how far down we would go or if we would survive. But, as God would have it, the car came to a sudden, jolting, stop, right side up.

The first thing I felt was the sensation of cool rain falling on my face through the car's smashed out windows. I was still alive! You never realize how safe you are, until your protection is suddenly and violently removed. Our belongings had been thrown from the car and lay all around us, yet we had been left seat-belted inside and miraculously unhurt. Aside from the fact that my nephew had just totaled his future father-in-law's new Alfa Romeo, no harm was done. Though our tumble down a mountainside ended well, it was terrifying.

On the other hand, on many occasions I have actually paid lots of money to be jostled around. Theme parks across the world are packed with eager participants who venture onto thrilling and seemingly dangerous rides. Instead of screaming in terror, we screech with delight as we precariously dangle hundreds of feet above the ground or miss colliding with certain death by mere inches.

The difference between these two experiences boils down to one simple word: trust. Because we trust that the theme-park equipment has passed the necessary safety requirements, we relax and enjoy; as soon as the ride is over we often get back in line for one more turn.

But what if one day, as we were waiting in line, a person was thrown from the ride, with his mangled body landing at our feet? Would we decide to get on that ride anyway? No one would; we would be crazy to do so. Even if the ride supervisor attempted to explain that the accident was a fluke and that it could never happen again, no one would go on that ride. In fact, some people would begin to question the safety of every other ride in the park.

The day trip would be over, but the ramifications could last for years. If the accident was significantly horrific, we may never try a thrill ride again. We might not just be done for the day; we might be done for the rest of our lives.

A serious breech of trust changes all perceptions. We have each seen the kind of trauma a breach of trust can bring upon an unsuspecting life, in relationship breakdowns, sporting and transportation accidents, and tragedies of all kinds. What once was greeted with wide-eyed anticipation is now a haunting memory.

This type of jarring experience keeps many people from loving the life that remains. God is blamed, vows are made, curses are activated, fear comes in, and faith takes flight. Just as we all sin and fall short of God's best for our lives, we each also battle a deep, underlying sense of failure. Unforgiven sins, an unhealed past, and unknown tomorrows paralyze most people on the planet, leaving them unable or unwilling to experience the many blessings God intended.

We don't have to understand what is going on in order to feel better—we just have to trust. If an unwavering trust can be restored and our confidence re-established, we will return to the joy of the journey.

All of us have read about or known people who have revisited their greatest fears in order to conquer them. They refused to allow past hurts to permanently mar their experience of life. Many of the people we consider heroes today hold that place in our hearts because they refused to give up.

Today, each of us faces this very same challenge. The sinless Lamb once again yearns to take our trust relationship to new heights. Every doorway to our future is purposefully designed to be entered with child-like faith; with arms reaching high into the air, completely confident and captivated by the Faithful One.

He will not fail us. He never has.

We have misinterpreted our past struggles and blamed an innocent God. It is time to cast our fears aside, disregard past misunderstandings, and rejoice in the God who is. We must wrap our arms around the only completely trustworthy Person in existence. Who, whether we realize it or not, is the only One who has never failed us. We finally grasp what life is all about when at last we realize God has always been there for us and always will be.[313]

NEW IS BETTER

During the 1930 Rose Bowl football game between the University of Southern California and Michigan, Michigan fumbled the ball. A USC player named Roy Rigel recovered it and, to the shock and horror of his teammates, Roy picked the ball up and began to run the wrong way. Not just for a few yards but, like a man possessed, Roy ran for 95 yards. It wasn't until just before he reached the wrong goal line that he was tackled by one of his own men. Michigan scored, which turned out to be the winning point.

At halftime, Roy sat by himself on the floor with a towel over his head and tears in his eyes, completely devastated. He had done the unthinkable! He had run the wrong way!

At the end of halftime, his coach said he wanted the same men who played the first half to go out and start the second. Roy sat there as if he hadn't heard a word. Finally,

WE HAVE MISINTERPRETED OUR PAST STRUGGLES AND BLAMED AN INNOCENT GOD.

his coach looked directly at him and insisted, "Roy, didn't you hear what I said? The same men who played the first half are going to start the second!"

WE ARE CALLED TO BUILD WHAT HAS NEVER BEEN BUILT BEFORE. OUT OF THE ASHES OF THE MORAL, SOCIAL, ECONOMIC, POLITICAL, AND SPIRITUAL DEMISE OF OUR SOCIETY WILL EMERGE THE CHURCH TRIUMPHANT.

It is recorded that Roy Rigel went out and played one of the most fierce and aggressive halves of football in USC history. He just needed one thing: a second chance.

All of us are looking for a second half, another shot; one more opportunity to make up for the mistakes of the first half. Today, receive God's second chance; receive the gracious prodding of the One who has never given up on you. He has already covered our mistakes in His precious blood and forgotten our sins.

"Remember the good old days!" Whoever came up with that statement must have had a bad memory. Which would you prefer, the old man or the new man; the old covenant or the new covenant? There has always been a conflict between the old and the new. That's why Jesus said, "You can't put new wine in old wineskins" or "new patches on old clothes."[314] He backed this up with His own example, giving those who had been swamped with old commandments one all-important new one: to love one another.[315]

We were created particularly to like new things. God, Himself, is so interested in new things that He has promised to make us a new Heaven and a new Earth. The same God who got a kick out of creating the universe instilled in us a deep appreciation for that which is fresh, clean, and new. We like new clothes, new hairstyles, new homes, and new cars. No one goes shopping with the hope of buying a worn-out car or a moth-eaten, fifth-generation jacket.

I am not knocking what is old. Age often has a majesty; an elegance; a nostalgia. But without reservation, I am convinced that new is better. Life is always new. Would anyone want to give birth to an old baby? Never! When a baby is born, it's brand, spanking new.

"Behold, I will do a new thing, now it shall spring forth; shall you not know it? I will even make a road in the wilderness, and rivers in the desert."[316] Aren't many Christians wandering through a wilderness and desert? That's not God's intent! " 'For I know the plans I have for you,' says the Lord. 'They are plans for good and not for disaster, to give you a future and a hope.' "[317] Perhaps you personally need a new job, a new house, a new body, a new perspective, a new vision, a new purpose, a new outlook on life, or a new relationship with God, His Word, and prayer. God alone has the spare parts for all of your needs.

Where are you? Do you find yourself settling for the mediocre, the predictable? Does the faith which once inflamed your imagination now taste like stale toast or soggy Cheerios? Have yesterday's failures dulled your hope for tomorrow? I'd rather have hotels on Mediterranean and Baltic, than be stuck with the mortgages on Boardwalk and Park Place! I'd rather be given a clean slate, a fresh start, than make one more feeble attempt at repairing the un-repairable.

We are called to build what has never been built before. Out of the ashes of the moral, social, economic, political, and spiritual demise of our society will emerge the Church Triumphant. That's why God is offering us a new beginning, and why He's even provided the recipe: "Purge out the old leaven, that you may be a new lump."[318] If we are willing to give up the old, God is eager to make our lives new. Give up your old, tired, troubled perspective. Trade it in for the mind of Christ. Jesus said, "The words that I speak to you are spirit, and they are life."[319] Let the Word of God become the life for which your soul longs.

THE GOD OF NEW BEGINNINGS

Once a year, at midnight, a strange ritual takes place. In homes, hotels, Elks Clubs and pool halls, a shout goes up all over the world—"Happy New Year!" The Earth begins another long lap around the sun, giving people 365 more days to live up to a new set of resolutions.

So what's the big deal? If no one told us that 12:00:01 AM on January 1st was such an enormous event, I doubt we'd notice any astronomical change. One year would simply fade into the next. Time would be an endless loop, punctuated only by the jumps we make from one waist size to the next.

Our New Year's enthusiasm is another indelible sign we are created in the image of a merciful God—the God of New Beginnings. Aren't you glad He isn't the God of Old Endings? Our Lord is unquestionably more concerned with tomorrow than He is with yesterday. That's why He has slated finite time for now and infinite time—the eternal tomorrow—for later. God describes what is taking place down here as a vapor, a moment;[320] in Heaven things are everlasting and never-ending. Everything up there is forever new—new bodies; new surroundings; even new names. Yet, the joys of tomorrow must be accessed by faith today.

"Every desirable and beneficial gift comes out of Heaven. The gifts are rivers of light cascading down from the Father of Light. There is nothing deceitful in God, nothing two-faced, nothing fickle."[321]

God stands as a lovesick bridegroom, standing at the door of our hearts, knocking ever so gently. Can you hear Him? Do you trust Him? Do you believe He is the fulfillment of all your dreams? A step of faith will invite Him into every corner of your heart and will lead to the eternal peace you have always longed for.

Step into eternity. Let the fears of yesterday be eclipsed by the faith of today and the hope of tomorrow. A change of mind is all that is needed; surrendering to the loving will of a benevolent God. Your best days are ahead, if you want them to be. That was God's plan from the beginning, and His flawless will for your life. Now, you have to decide if it is your will.

SUMMARY POINTS

- Every irritation is an invitation to go to the next level. Frustrations are veiled doorways to our destiny. If we obsess over the pain and displeasure inherently associated with the struggles of life, we will miss the entire point.

- There are no coincidences in God, only opportunities. Absolutely everything we have gone through in life has prepared us for the God-conceived opportunities and challenges ahead.

- We are each continually positioned for success. All that is needed is for our hearts to remain open and trusting, surrendered to the One greater than our meager little plans. We must continually remind ourselves how invaluable, even priceless, we are to our heavenly Father. Behind every challenging circumstance, there is a loving God whose victorious perspective is far greater than the trial we face.

- If you are bored, it is not God's fault. Boredom is a result of being unable or unwilling to see life from God's perspective.

QUESTIONS FOR DISCUSSION

1. Reflect on a recent irritation in your life. How was it an invitation to the next level of your growth and maturity? How did you respond? In what ways could you have responded better? How do you think that would have affected you?

2. In what areas of your life were you recently at risk in your life? Who was holding your rope? How were they able to help you? Could they have helped you better? In what ways are you holding the rope in someone else's life?

3. In what ways has God shown you new perspectives about your life during this study?

4. Old things in our life have to make room for the new things. What new thing is God doing in your heart? What kind of access are you giving God to your heart? What benefit do the old things have? What benefit do the new things have? What are some strategies for change that God is giving you?

5. What has impacted you the most during this 12 chapter study? How have your thoughts and feelings changed about God, yourself, and others? How has this affected your life?

ENDNOTES

71	1 Kings 1:29
72	Acts 13:22b
73	Ecclesiastes 2:17
74	Micah 6:7
75	Galatians 6:7
76	Daniel 4:33
77	Psalm 37:18
78	I have included a copy of my mom's prayer in the Appendix.
79	Psalms 46:10
80	1 Corinthians 15:31
81	Romans 8:11
82	Philippians 3:7–8, 10–11

CHAPTER 5

83	Proverbs 22:6
84	Hebrews 12:2, *NLT*
85	John 15:13
86	Luke 7:39
87	Luke 7:47
88	Philippians 1:20b–21
89	Psalms 17:15
90	John 12:24–25
91	Colossians 3:3, *NLT*
92	Colossians 3:1–2
93	Matthew 19:30
94	John 6:53
95	John 6:54–56
96	John 6:60–61
97	John 6:66
98	1 Corinthians 13:3

99	Oswald Chambers, *My Utmost For His Highest,* June 16TH
100	Isaiah 53:3–5
101	Mark 14:32–34
102	Mark 14:35–36
103	1 Timothy 1:15
104	2 Corinthians 5:21
105	1 John 1:5
106	Ephesians 5:11
107	Acts 20:22–23
108	Acts 20:24
109	1 Corinthians 2:9–10a

CHAPTER 6

110	Luke 11:23
111	1 John 1:5–7
112	2 Corinthians 2:11
113	John 15:15
114	Mark 14:21
115	2 Corinthians 3:2
116	Psalm 107:2
117	1 John 3:8b
118	Revelation 20:10
119	Revelation 12:11
120	Revelation 13:8
121	Luke 19:40
122	John 8:44
123	Hebrews 4:13
124	Luke 11:33–34
125	John 14:30

126   1 Corinthians 11:1

127   Psalms 107:20

128   Luke 4:17–19

129   John Toland, *Adolph Hitler,*
      Volume I (Garden City: Doubleday
      and Company Inc.) p. 3, 8

130   Ruth 1:16b

131   Colossians 1:27

132   Philippians 2:3

133   Song of Solomon 3:1–2, 4

134   Song of Solomon 5:8

135   Song of Solomon 6:8–9

136   1 Corinthians 1:18

137   1 John 1:5–7

138   John 9:5

153   1 Peter 5:7

154   Philippians 4:6

155   Hebrews 5:8, *NLT*

156   Malcolm Muggeridge,
      in *Homemade*, July, 1990

157   Romans 8:37

158   2 Corinthians 7:4

159   Oswald Chambers,
      My Utmost For His Highest,
      March 7TH

160   Psalms 116:7

161   2 Corinthians 7:4

162   2 Corinthians 12:9

163   Psalm 121:1

164   Romans 8:18

CHAPTER 7

139   Proverbs 25:2

140   Psalms 37:25a, *NLT*

141   Exodus 33:11

142   Isaiah 55:8–9

143   2 Corinthians 4:16–17

144   2 Corinthians 2:14

145   Proverbs 23:7

146   Psalms 55:22

147   1 Kings 1:29

148   2 Samuel 4:9

149   1 Samuel 17

150   1 Samuel 21

151   1 Samuel 22–23

152   2 Samuel 15:10–13

CHAPTER 8

165   2 Corinthians 7:4

166   Psalms 30:5b

167   1 Peter 1:8

168   Hebrews 12:2b

169   James 1:2–4

170   Ephesians 5:18, *NLT*

171   For more information see the book
      One Witness by Aggie Hurst.

172   Psalms 16:11

173   1 Peter 4:12–13

174   Mike Bickle, *The Pleasures*
      of Loving God, 55–56

175   1 Peter 4:19

176   Colossians 3:1–2

177 2 Corinthians 2:14

178 2 Timothy 1:12

179 2 Corinthians 6:1

180 2 Peter 1:3a, *NLT*

181 Psalms 31:9–10

182 Psalms 31:7

183 1 Corinthians 15:58

184 Psalms 61:2

185 1 Peter 4:19

186 1 Corinthians 10:13

CHAPTER 9

187 Acts 7:56

188 Oswald Chambers,
     My Utmost For His Highest,
     August 2ND

189 1 Peter 5:5b

190 Isaiah 14:14

191 Acts 10:34

192 Esther 2:14, Isaiah 56:4,
     Jeremiah 38:7, Daniel 1:7–11

193 *World English Dictionary*

194 Acts 8:27–39

195 Psalms 139:15

196 Psalms 139:14

197 Proverbs 3:5

198 Psalms 118:8

199 Psalms 40:4

200 Psalms 5:11

201 Luke 14:33, *The Message*

202 Matthew 12:33

203 John 3:3–7

204 Joshua 33:11

205 Matthew 7:21–23

206 Song 1:4a

207 John 12:27

208 Romans 8:29

209 Genesis 1:26

210 2 Corinthians 1:8

211 Philippians 4:18

212 Philippians 1:21

213 Hebrews 12:2

214 1 Corinthians 15:31

215 1 Peter 1:6, *NLT*

216 John 11:35

217 1 Thessalonians 5:16

218 Revelation 21:4

219 Isaiah 53:3

220 Mark 4:21

221 Matthew 23:24

222 Matthew 7:3

223 Matthew 8:22

224 Matthew 7:6

225 Mark 10:25

226 Matthew 16:18

227 Proverbs 15:15

228 Matthew 6:10

229 Luke 16:29–31

230 Luke 17:17–18

231 Oswald Chambers,
     My Utmost For His Highest,
     Feb. 7TH

232   Romans 14:10, 2 Corinthians 5:10

233   Romans 1:20

234   Philippians 4:8

235   Psalm 87:7

236   Revelation 22:1

237   Luke 17:21

238   John 7:38, *NLT*

239   Revelation 22:17, *NLT*

CHAPTER 10

240   Ecclesiastes 3:11

241   Hebrews 11:13–16

242   Leviticus 20:24

243   Amos 9:14

244   Genesis 50:20

245   Matthew 17:20b

246   Oswald Chambers,
      My Utmost For His Highest,
      July 29TH

247   1 John 1:5

248   James 4:8

249   John 17:24

250   John 15:9

251   1 John 3:1

252   Genesis 39:23

253   Job 42:12

254   1 Samuel 18:14

255   Romans 8:29

256   Revelation 3:12

257   2 Timothy 2:13

258   John 16:33

259   Colossians 3:3

260   Romans 8:35–37

261   Matthew 10:24

262   Revelation 3:17b

263   Hebrews 4:13b

264   John 9:41

CHAPTER 11

265   Oswald Chambers,
      My Utmost For His Highest,
      July 28TH

266   John 15:1–2, 4–5

267   John 15:8

268   Ephesians 5:8

269   Psalms 56:13

270   Proverbs 4:23

271   John 10:10

272   Luke 12:48b

273   1 Corinthians 16:9

274   Oswald Chambers,
      My Utmost For His Highest,
      January 13TH

275   Luke 18:17

276   2 Corinthians 11:27;
      2 Corinthians 6:5

277   Matthew 4:3–4

278   Philippians 3:19

279   John 4:32

280   John 4:34

281   Genesis 1:1–2

282   Genesis 1:2

283   Proverbs 27:7, *NLT*

284   1 John 1:6

285   John 3:19, *The Message*

286   Ephesians 5:8a

287   Revelation 22:2

288   Matthew 6:34

289   2 Samuel 11:1–2

290   Genesis 3

291   Jeremiah 8:7, *NLT*

292   John 13:37–38

293   Oswald Chambers,
       My Utmost For His Highest,
       June 29ᵀᴴ

294   1 Timothy 3:6

295   John 15:1–2

296   Hebrews 12:11b

297   Psalms 51:6

298   1 Corinthians 5:7

310   Matthew 11:30

311   Philippians 1:6

312   Ephesians 3:20

313   Matthew 28:20

314   Matthew 9:17

315   I John 4:7–8

316   Isaiah 43:19

317   Jeremiah 29:11

318   1 Corinthians 5:7

319   John 6:63b

320   1 Corinthians 15:52

321   James 1:17, *The Message*

CHAPTER 12

299   Colossians 1:13, NLT

300   Hebrews 12:11

301   Philippians 1:12, *Amplified*

302   Luke 18:27, *NLT*

303   Psalms 121:3

304   Ephesians 1:18, *NLT*

305   Job 36:12, *NLT*

306   Genesis 3:10

307   Matthew 10:29–31

308   Matthew 6:34

309   Philippians 3:11–12, *NLT*

SMALL GROUP GUIDELINES

Small groups are one of the most effective ways that God can use to bring healing into our lives. In a small group we are able to share transparently and be loved unconditionally. However, if done incorrectly, small groups can also be one of the most hurtful places for a person. Below are a few guidelines to help your small group be successful. Before you begin, please make sure that all participants agree with the following statements:

I will keep everything that is shared in the group confidential.

I will listen respectfully to others thoughts and feelings (resisting the urge to give advice unless solicited).

I will strive to be personally transparent and accepting of the transparency of others.

I will strive to be accountable (use "I statements).

I will help keep the discussions focused.

APPENDIX B

THE PRAYER MINISTRY OF FRANCES ANFUSO

Frances Anfuso is the mother of Pastor Francis Anfuso. She went to be with the Lord in 1997, at the age of 91. Because of her prayers, Francis received the Lord on Mother's Day, 1972. All of her five children are saved and actively serving the Lord.

Nana prayed the below written prayer an average of four hours per day for ten years. During the peak of her intercessory ministry, she prayed for hundreds of unsaved loved ones on one day, and hundreds of Christians the next.

People would call her from all over America to get on her prayer list.

NANA'S PRAYER

I claim _____ as God's purchased possession, in the name of Jesus Christ, on the basis of Your shed blood.

I claim the tearing down of all the works of Satan in _____'s life; all false doctrine, unbelief, temporal values, hatred, resentment, bitterness, and deceitfulness.

I claim that each of _____'s thoughts will be brought into captivity to the obedience of Jesus Christ.

I claim the complete deliverance of _____ from the power and persuasion of the devil.

I pray that _____ will be brought into submission, and that his (her) conscience will be convicted and brought to the point of repentance.

I pray that _____ will hear and believe God's Word, and that God's will and purpose will be accomplished in and through _____'s life.

Thank you, Jesus, for hearing and answering my prayer!

NINE KEY POINTS

1. Claim each person by name as God's purchased possession.

2. In the name of the Lord Jesus Christ, on the basis of His shed blood.

3. Claim the tearing down of the works of Satan in his or her life (false doctrine, unbelief, temporal values, hatred, resentment, bitterness, deceitfulness)

4. Claim that each thought (of the person) is being brought into captivity to the obedience of Jesus Christ.

5. Claim the complete deliverance of the person from the power and persuasion of the devil.

6. Pray they will be brought into submission and their conscience to be convicted.

7. Pray that he will be brought to the point of repentance.

8. Pray that he will hear and believe God's Word.

9. Pray that God's will and purpose will be accomplished in and through his life.

INDEX